I0761658

The S@#t I've Heard at Yoga

The S@#t I've Heard at Yoga

(what I learned in downward dog)

Michael J. Norton

PERMUTED PRESS

A PERMUTED PRESS BOOK
ISBN: 979-8-89565-236-7
ISBN (eBook): 979-8-89565-237-4

The S@#t I've Heard at Yoga:
What I Learned in Downward Dog

Cover design by Barbara Aronica

This book, as well as any other Post Hill Press publications, may be purchased in bulk quantities at a special discounted rate. Contact orders@posthillpress.com for more information.

All people, locations, events, and situations are portrayed to the best of the author's memory. While all of the events described are true, many names and identifying details have been changed to protect the privacy of the people involved.

Permuted Press
New York • Nashville
permutedpress.com

Published in the United States of America
1 2 3 4 5 6 7 8 9 10

Randall and Cookie

For listening to my s@#t as we wander through life.

TABLE OF CONTENTS

"YOU SEEM SO CALM."....1
"YOU'RE NOT REALLY RELAXED, ARE YOU?"....6

FROM THE MOUTH OF YOGIS

"SO, I SAID TO MYSELF, 'SHUT UP!'"....15
"THERE ARE SQUIRRELS RUNNING AROUND INSIDE YOUR HEAD."....18
"EVERY TIME YOU JUDGE YOURSELF, YOU BREAK YOUR OWN HEART."....20
"ARE YOU AN EX-SOMETHING, OR ARE YOU YOUR NEXT SOMETHING?"..22
"HE STARTED YOGA AT EIGHTY-FIVE?!"....25
"YOUR BODY WILL NEVER DO WHAT IT DIDN'T LEARN TO DO THIRTY YEARS AGO."....30
"DO NOT LAMENT THE THINGS YOU CAN'T CONTROL."....34
"BE A BEGINNER."....36
"EVEN FLOWERS KNOW TO TURN TO THE LIGHT."....38
"YOU CAN'T THINK YOUR WAY OUT OF IT."....41
"IF YOU FEEL OVERWHELMED, JUST DO THE NEXT RIGHT THING."....44
"WHEN YOU WANT POWER, YOU HAVE NONE."....47
"CALM IS THE NEW POWER."....53
"BE BATTLE READY."....55
"WHAT'S THE MOST INTERESTING THING ABOUT YOU?"....58
"CHER CAN HOLD A PLANK POSE FOR FIVE MINUTES."....65
"WE BEND SO WE DON'T BREAK."....68

"DO LESS. ALLOW MORE." 69
"UN-RAZZLE-DAZZLE YOURSELVES." 72
"DON'T OVERACHIEVE." 76
"KNOW LESS." 80
"KEEP WHAT YOU LOVE." 82
"SMART PEOPLE KEEP IT SIMPLE." 84
"APPRECIATION OF WHAT YOU HAVE IS THE BEST PROFIT IN LIFE." 87
"WE'RE GOING TO MAKE LOVE TO OUR JOINTS. DO YOU LOVE YOUR BIG TOE ENOUGH?" 90
"LET'S GET OUR BODY READY FOR THE RAIN." 91
"BE CAREFUL NOT TO SPEND TOO MUCH TIME IN THE PAST. IT WAS NEVER WHAT YOU REMEMBER." 92
"UNCLOUD." 94
"APPRECIATE WHAT YOU GET, NOT WHAT YOU DON'T GET." 96
"WE'LL BEGIN IN FIVE." 98
"WHAT YOU RESIST WILL PERSIST!" 99
"IT'S OKAY TO BE AFRAID, BUT YOU DON'T HAVE TO REACT TO IT." 104
"ORGANIZE YOUR FACE." 107
"NOTHINGNESS. CAN YOU GET THERE?" 109
"NOTHINGNESS IS MY NEW NEW YEAR'S RESOLUTION!" 113
"A FART." 120
"CLOSE YOUR EYES SO YOU'RE NOT COMPARING YOURSELF TO OTHERS IN THE ROOM." 121
"WHEN DOES TIME SLOW DOWN?" 123
"DON'T FORCE A POSE." 125
"NAMASTE." 128

THE YOGA COOLDOWN

"THIS PLACE SHOULD BE A SITCOM." 133
"YOU EAT CHEESE?" 135
"THEY DRIVE ME CRAZY." 138
"HEY, BUDDY—YOU KNOW WHERE TO GET MY PHONE FIXED?" 139
"MOM FUCKED UP YOGA." 144
"WHAT'S NEW?" 152

"YOU KNOW THAT'S A CRAZY PRICE FOR A LOAF OF BREAD." 155
"HAVE YOU EVER DONE YOUR BRAND SHIT ON YOURSELF?" 160
"DO SOMETHING THAT SCARES YOU." 164
"YOU SHOULD WRITE A BOOK!" 169
TXT CHAIN: March 2020 172
"CAN I WRITE A BOOK?" 174
"WHO NEEDS OR WANTS THIS BOOK?" 182
"THINK ABOUT WHAT YOU CAN DO, NOT WHAT YOU CAN'T DO." 188
"OMG! WHAT EXACTLY IS THE POINT OF ALL THIS?" 190
"WE SHOULD GET TOGETHER…" 192
"SHIRTLESS IN A SNOWSTORM (and the dawn of my ennui)." 196
"I WANT TO BE ANDY-HAPPY." 203

DRIVE TIME

"CUTE BRAS FOR WOMEN OVER FIFTY?" 213
"WHEN CAN I GET FAT?" 220
"RAY SEEMS HAPPY." 226
"I BLAME EVERYTHING ON HILLARY CLINTON!" 231

LIVING THE CHANGE

"AFTER SIXTY…" 241
"MIND THE MUDDLE." 245
"THAT WAS A LOT OF FASHION FOR A YOGA CLASS." 249
"ALEC BALDWIN LOOKS…" 253
"I NEED A NEW BRAND!" 256
"THAT'S THAT." 259

THE BLAH, BLAH, BLAH ABOUT ME

"WHO AM I ANYWAY?" 263
ACKNOWLEDGMENTS 269
ABOUT THE AUTHOR 271

"YOU SEEM SO CALM."

I kept hearing this, even though at my core, I was unsettled.

Both friends and strangers have lobbed this random comment my way over the past few years. For most of my life, I was never a calm person, at least on the inside. I dressed the part of "guy in control"—always put together. I may have navigated the day with a certain amount of sartorial confidence, but I was a host for stomach knots, sweaty nerves, and Tums-popping nights. My brain was like a Jiffy Pop of anxiety. I spent many sleepless nights watching time tick away on the clock.

You seem calm.

Yes. I'd even said that to myself....

When did "calm" happen? How did it happen? When did I shift?

When did my husband start getting jealous of my ability to fall asleep and stay asleep?

When did clarity begin to outweigh confusion?

When did I stop squandering time and emotion on friends who served up no nutritional value?

When did my essence evolve from closeted insecurity to visible calm?

I wasn't running my life like a race. I wasn't calculating the value of every decision as a deposit into some amorphous idea of happiness.

Idling in summer traffic, hoping to get to a movie in Sag Harbor on time, a friend noted, "You really are...much calmer."

"You've said that before."

"Yeah. And direct. You're much more direct."

With focused scrutiny and reflection, I offer up: "Could be that shit I hear at yoga."

If this shift is real, it is because I've transformed with the emotional, physical, and spiritual codes of my Amagansett yogis. I didn't just hear them; I *felt* them. And that's in spite of the Kevlar-strength cynicism I developed as a Catholic school boy.

In the midst of a pointless week in the bleakness of late November, 2020, I start constructing the year-end review I always give myself. I ruminate on next year's goals.

> ME: I've been thinking a lot about how often in life we need to change, evolve, reinvent, rethink, rebrand, or reimagine life as we live it.
>
> OLD ME: Don't!
>
> ME: Don't what?
>
> OLD ME: Write a book.
>
> ME: I never said anything about writing a book.
>
> OLD ME: Remember, I always know what you're thinking.
>
> ME: You know, you could be more supportive."
>
> OLD ME: "Supportive of what?"
>
> ME: "Well, you could at least listen to my idea."
>
> OLD ME: "The great gay novel?"
>
> ME: "No. Hanya Yanagihara already did that. More like a book about rethinking your life."
>
> OLD ME: "Like self-help?"
>
> ME: "No—hopefully funnier than self-help."

OLD ME: "Yet another humorous essayist?"

ME: "I refuse to participate in this negativity."

That night, at 3:47 am to be exact, my inner critic woke me up in a snit demanding to be heard:

OLD ME: "Stop right now! You can't write a book about yoga, so don't even think it."

ME: Why not?

OLD ME: Yes, you practice yoga, but no one would look at you and say, "Yogi." You've never had a top knot. You're not lean. You're not that flexible—physically or emotionally. You're not a plant-based person. And you were raised Catholic, so you're more superstitious than spiritual.

ME: Lots of people have commented on how calm I appear to be.

OLD ME: People on Trazodone are calm too.

ME: "You're exhausting to be around."

OLD ME: "Calm—so what? But really, are you happy? Be honest," old me challenges with a snide sense of superiority.

ME: "I think I am…."

OLD ME: "Not new-sweater happy, but really happy?"

I sense the old me is jealous of the new me.

ME: "I'm not even thinking it'll get published."

OLD ME: "Then why?"

ME: "Just for me. I'm doing it for me."

OLD ME: "Fine. Write your book. What else are you and every other self-involved creative person going to do during this lockdown?"

ME: "Your negativity definitely goes in the threat quadrant of my personal SWOT analysis."

OLD ME: "Sorry—I'm a strength. A robust inner critic will always be your best editor, saving you from the bad ideas made possible by our privilege…."

ME: "I get it. I read *Caste* and *White Fragility*…."

OLD ME: "So, you know luck of the draw worked really hard for you? You'll be fresh meat on social media. You ready for that?"

ME: "Avoidance is never a winning strategy."

OLD ME: "It is in dodgeball. And Instagram comments."

ME: "If we weren't the same person, I'd never talk to you again."

I don't know how many how-to books the world needs, but I do know there's an endless supply of people looking for solutions and shortcuts to solving their shit.

There's advice everywhere. Friends, colleagues, Instagram gurus, and therapy apps offer a bounty of interesting, provocative, and insightful easy-does-it strategies for just about every human condition. Lots of us collect inspiring tidbits from grandmothers, favorite teachers, or random waiting room conversations.

People love to share their stories, both their dramas and their victories.

Maybe you had an enlightening encounter with a New Zealander while enduring a travel delay at LAX? Or a random but meaningful exchange with a Jill Sander addict in a Barney's dressing room? (Back when there was a Barney's.) Or what about an "OMG me too!" heart-to-heart moment in Starbucks with a stranger who, in the moment, felt like a newfound forever-friend? There can be wisdom in these moments, but those insights are often lost to the speed of life.

We, the people, are living longer. To thrive, we can't just run in place for the rest of our lives. We job jump and career change more frequently. We shift behavior and expectations with the constant parade of technological innovations. We quickly developed the language of emoticoms so we can communicate at the speed of text. Climate crisis demands that we rethink how we live in the world. We must evolve, seemingly on a daily basis. It's what our species has always done. It's why we can walk upright, play pickleball, and navigate life with a latte in one hand and a phone in the other.

Reinvention is a tool for survival. It's how businesses evolve to sync with dynamic markets. It's how brands maintain cultural relevance. And at those moments when life gives you lemons—when you feel stuck in who you are today—with thoughtful choices and a strong sense of self, the next you is waiting to show up and take your place.

I've enjoyed a huge internal shift—a downshift. I no longer live at the speed of life. I live in the world with different energy. I think, feel, respond, and react in a lower gear.

I didn't have to quit or change anything.

I didn't do a workshop or find myself at a spiritual retreat.

No ayahuasca for me.

No psychedelic-assisted therapy, although I'm intrigued.

No time with a psychiatrist.

I didn't read a here's-the-trick-to-life book.

I've spent no time with a transformative podcast.

I am more patient, but have no time for bullshit.

I'm more accepting, but have no interest in a waste of energy.

I sleep better. I now know that being well-rested is heaven on earth.

What happened?

It's definitely the shit I heard at yoga!

"YOU'RE NOT REALLY RELAXED, ARE YOU?"

INT. JACK'S COFFEE, AMAGANSETT – A MID-WEEK MORNING, 2015

I had recently left my job as Global Creative Director of Maybelline NY. It was a job I wanted to quit from day one. Beauty is not a pretty business. But today, I'm living my fantasy, the one I carried with me walking to work every day of my marketing career: a morning without the anticipation of any number of glitches that ad people elevate to "fucking disaster!"

I settle in with an email-free latte. No client stress. No ticking clock.

ME

(to me, mind racing)

You're not really relaxed, are you?
No. And I have a whole day of nothing!
You're not used to nothing.
And I'm not sure I want to get used to nothing.

An unknown number flashes on my phone.

ME

Let it go to voice mail. Probably another offer to spend three nights in a Marriot of my choice.

It's February, but it doesn't feel like winter. It's a February day pretending to be March 30. I, too, feel like I'm not in the right season of my life.

ME

It's another perfect day to review my entire life and neatly organize all of my regrets.

I conclude a warp-speed assessment of the past couple of decades with a breathtaking question.

ME

Was I really ever where I was supposed to be?

Yeah, now I'm a guy in a coffee shop with nothing to do. You're like a has-been in your own life.

Now what?

Uncertainty—it's that thief in the night. It creeps into the beds of everyone I know and steals our sleep…if we haven't taken a gummy. I know because I've asked.

"Now what?"

This simple question drives, haunts, and paralyzes everybody at some point in their life. It's often asked when staring down one of life's unexpected twists: a relationship crash, a painful loss, or a health setback. Maybe you hear that wretched *hiss* of the air leaking out of your career balloon.

"Now what?" can crush your energy on a landmark birthday, whether you're thirty or fifty or seventy. The person who you were is not who you are in the moment. These are moments to assess if you really are who you want to be. If the past feels better than the present, then you need to change that. "Now what?" moments can nudge you forward into the next phase of life and the next phase of you.

Maybe you're one of the lucky ones who can counter with, "What if I did everything right?"

Let's be honest, there are very few of you. Even if you've executed a perfectly crafted plan, waking up happy isn't guaranteed. You may, at some point, wonder if there is a plan B. Or if plan B should have been plan A. This book may reaffirm your current happiness or help you find the next you. I mean, if you did everything right, you should be happy… right? You are happy, aren't you?

Now what?

This played in my head like a Taylor Swift bridge waiting to be written.

Think this through.

I've been there before. I had a career bomb. A medical scare. I've been broke. I lost half my stuff in an earthquake.

Throughout our lives, as our big and small worlds shift, tumble, grow, and change, we need to respond, not just react.

Reaction = a defense, more emotional than thoughtful

Response = a commanding, informed, proactive decision

I didn't want a whole new life, but I wanted my life to feel new to me.

I didn't want to turn back time, but I didn't want to feel the weight of aging.

As I shed the skin of my old life, I didn't know who I was going to be.

I needed to see myself so I could be myself.

With shifts in career and energy, our purpose and passions can become ghosts.

With Botox, Fraxel, and CoolSculpting, you can fight the physical droops and blobs that haunt you in the mirror. I just wish my dermatologist could laser away the emotional sagging that comes with age.

Jack's Coffee was pretty chill that morning. It was just me. The barista was held captive by her phone. I savored that last foamy sip of my latte.

I left in silence—except for the screaming inside my head: *Now what, now what, now what?*

Headed to my car, I walked past a yoga studio. In the dim light, there was a forest of people holding themselves in tree pose. I felt like an intruder. I fled, as if I'd done something wrong.

I started the car and looked in the rearview mirror. The me I saw did not reflect my harried confusion in this moment. The me in the mirror knew something I'd yet to realize.

Now what? for me at that very moment was going back to yoga.

Yoga is where I went when I didn't know where else to go.

By the time the world screeched to halt in 2020, I'd been rewired by the tidbits of philosophy that bookended each class.

I started to write them all down. I needed to feel productive.

Then I decided to shape it into a more coherent presentation.

My "professor self" then said, "Give it personality. Always infuse your writing with a bit of you."

I hadn't planned on writing a book, but I wound up with this one.

So, for all those people who don't go to yoga, I decided to catalog all of the tidbits that might help them settle into a deeper shade of bliss.

Change is good.

I suspect there's something in here for everyone, even the lucky person who loves themself and everything about their life.

One suggestion: Every time you pick up this book to read another chapter, start with the sound of "om." I love the possibility that whenever someone on a plane, train, beach, or public bench opens this book, they fill their space with those primordial vibrations—a sound proven to promote calm and relaxation.

Let me ask this question *for* you: "Who are you, Michael? Why should I listen to you?"

Excellent question. There's a whole chapter about me at the end of the book. You can read that anytime you want to. But first, a tell about my true value as a colleague and friend.

INT. SAN AMBROES, MADISON AVENUE – 8:52 a.m.

A former boss stares across the table; it's the same bit of wonder and confusion that a child has assessing if this Santa Claus thing is for real.

FORMER BOSS

How do you do it?

ME

Do what?

FORMER BOSS

Get people to like you?

A careful silence.

The clients…they all seem to like you.

ME

Oh—that's easy. I listen.

An unnerving thought to a man who never stops talking.

In that moment, I discovered my true superpower: listening.

Clients love being heard. And don't we all?

While the rest of my species has dramatically increased their response time, steamrolling their way through conversation, I'm like a rabbit in the wild, always on high alert listening for the sound of predators.

In his book, *Outliers*, Malcolm Gladwell asserted that practicing a skill for ten thousand hours makes you an expert. Of course, the context is more about violinists and computer programmers, but, in short, I've put in ten thousand hours as a GBF (gay best friend), helping others work through the various dramas of every stage of life. I also teach branding and marketing at Parsons School of Design. In my first class of every term, I sum up the talent and job of a marketer with one slide:

"LEARN TO LISTEN TO THE WORLD"

I've put in my ten thousand hours as a brand strategist, analyzing the needs and desires of consumers in just about every slice of their life. As a marketer, you have to anticipate the future. Your holy grail is being where consumers are going before they get there.

Even though I don't have social media notoriety or a notable podcast, I listen intensely to the current howl of our culture.

Now, navigating the physical and emotional shifts of my sixties, I watch and listen more intently to people of all ages who get trapped in a stare down with the devil of uncertainty. I have an ongoing and often annoying dialogue with myself, interrogating why we do what we do and why we might feel what we feel.

So as you read this book, you can be sure that I listened with ears wide open to the shit I've heard at yoga. It's good stuff.

And so, my book begins....

Finally, right?

FROM THE MOUTH OF YOGIS

The shit I've heard in class.

"SO, I SAID TO MYSELF, 'SHUT UP!'"

When I first started yoga, I didn't pay attention to the teachers' "welcome, yogis, blah, blah, blah." These three minutes of inspiration, philosophies, and bits of wisdom always played like a cliché scene in a bad episode of *Seinfeld.* Yes, there are bad episodes of *Seinfeld*—season one was not good. Since I was using yoga to replace running, I impatiently indulged the spiritual musings, anxious to get to the exercise portion of the practice. I kept thinking, *What is this shit?*

I tried different teachers. They all had an opening monologue.

When are they going to stop talking!? I wondered.

After about ten classes, I accepted that I was "in the room" and that the class wasn't going to change simply because my inside voice was chanting, "Let's go let's go let's go." One day, while sitting in a facsimile of a relaxed pose, I was busy cataloguing the active grievances in my life. A breeze lifted the almost-weightless, gauze-like purple curtain, providing a glimpse into the leafy tranquility of Amagansett Square. A little girl, so small she still wobbled as she ran, chased after a puppy. Yes, a puppy! Was I living inside a Hallmark card designed for a special grandma? I punched back at the cynicism: Why couldn't something that cute, that simple, that playful, happen in real life?

I began to search my memory bank: Was there ever a moment like that in my childhood? Did the wobbly little me ever chase a puppy through the vibrant greens of a late spring day? Probably not. My father never trusted dogs. He was afraid of them. He could yell at his children and know for certain they would cower; he was always afraid a dog might bite back.

I learned early on to take my joy where I could find it—in my case, cuddly sweaters. Transfixed by that little girl in gigglish pursuit of her baby lab, my mind slowed, as if someone eased their foot onto the brakes of my thought processor. Accidentally, I heard softly spoken guidance floating through the room.

ME (silently, to myself): Shut up and listen.

Something about squirrels in my head? Wait—was that an unexpected whiff of relevance? My mind downshifted. A prick of curiosity. I was finally "in the room." I was "present." Settled. Was I on my way to some sort of om-infused enlightenment? A soft wave of laughter moved through the room—a nod to the collective recognition of a truth? My curiosity was piqued. Everyone seemed to be glowing just a bit. What did I miss?

The next class, I showed up with my ears on. I embraced active listening. I came with the expectation of being lifted by the power of magical, mystical insights. If there was gold to mine in the opening monologue, that gold was going to be mine. I had my hands in prayer position and I was all set to get rich quick.

Some of what I heard began to resonate. It was shit I needed to hear. I was learning a new language, not for communicating with others, but as a way of connecting with myself. A way of being in the world. My world.

The physical benefits of yoga are different than the benefits of a six-mile run. Yoga stretched my body; changed my posture; and built strength, stamina, and balance. However, it's the little "spiritual bits" that helped shape who I've become. They've strengthened the equally important emotional muscles: patience, calm, acceptance, and confidence. There is less noise in my head, so I'm more present in my life. I'm more at ease with uncertainty.

Hey, reader, did you just roll your eyes? That's okay.

Just a few years ago, if you told me you were "more present in your life," you would have heard my eyeballs hit the back of my head. I don't roll my eyes anymore. That doesn't make me a better person, but it makes me a happier person. I'm much calmer than my pre-yoga days. We've all heard the saying, "If I knew then what I know now…." Well, this "shit" I picked up at yoga is *exactly* the shit I wish I knew then.

So stay with me. Shut up and listen. Not to me, but to what I heard and learned along the way to "namaste."

"THERE ARE SQUIRRELS RUNNING AROUND INSIDE YOUR HEAD."

Cynicism is my strongest muscle, but when I heard this squirrel thing, I thought, *I have to remember that!*

All through the sun salutations and downward dogs, I kept thinking *squirrels, squirrels, squirrels,* but of course, as soon as I left class, I immediately forgot what I was supposed to remember.

I arrived at my next class determined to reap the rewards of active listening. Walking through the parking lot, I was being my own best coach: *Be more present. More conscious.*

There was a scrum of ponytails and leggings waiting for the previous class to empty the room. I amuse myself, *You've arrived at the Church of Lululemon.*

My teacher stepped outside for a big inhale of fresh air just as I reached the door. *Opportunity—take it.*

ME: "Last week…you said something about squirrels?"

TEACHER: "The squirrels running around in your head."

ME: "Yes!"

TEACHER: "They make you nuts."

ME: "Yes! So, it's not just me?"

TEACHER: "Nothing in this world is ever just you."

ME: "Mic drop!"

This is said way too much, but this truly was a mic drop!

Squirrels running around in my head! It is the perfect metaphor. They're the reason I feverishly bit my fingernails my entire life. In really anxious times, I should have had hyperbaric oxygen therapy to remedy the damage I had done to my fingers. Having this new image of devil-eyed squirrels careening around my psyche, I suddenly felt less nuts (pun intended).

Squirrels! Who doesn't love a little anthropomorphism? Turning my unnamed emotional twisters into bushy-tailed cartoons somehow reduced their power over me. Squirrels can scratch your eyes out, but for the most part, they run up a tree as soon as you get too close.

A week before, when the yogi mentioned those "squirrels," there was a room full of recognition.

I couldn't imagine that other people also juggled multiple balls of angst inside their heads.

I couldn't imagine other people woke up in the middle of the night wanting to rewrite conversations they had earlier that day.

Could it be that other people idling at eight-lane intersections were also reliving moments of regret from twenty years ago?

Aha! I wasn't alone. At least when I was at yoga.

I wasn't swimming in anxiety. When I was at yoga.

I was learning. At yoga.

"EVERY TIME YOU JUDGE YOURSELF, YOU BREAK YOUR OWN HEART."

Truth. You know it when you hear it.

"I see lots of head nods around the room. We all do it, right? We spend too much time telling ourselves we don't measure up to something. To someone. What? Who?"

I wanted to raise my hand. I wanted to share. I wanted to tell the whole class, "I get into bed every night regretting something stupid and unintentional I said to someone that day."

My heart breaks every time I replay my foot-in-mouth moment of the day.

If you've never seen the 2001 French film, *Amelie*, you might want to check it out. Or you can just google the scene where Amelie melts. Type "Amelie melts" into your browser. It's a five-second clip. When I heard, "Every time you judge yourself, you break your own heart," I melted just like Amelie. That simple truth unlocked every muscle that allegedly made me strong. I've lived my whole life breaking my own heart. I had an "Amelie melt" almost every day.

Most people are never as good looking as they want to be. As popular as they hope to be. Very few have everything they've ever wanted. Our judgment of ourselves is the cruelest and most crippling energy we face. It is emotional cancer. Just like smoking, it's a nasty habit and, it's time to quit it.

And about that, there's nothing more to say.

With the collective recognition of the yoga class, I felt better knowing it wasn't just me. Why do we think that we're the only ones who are broken? Self-improvement is a $10 billion business. That's a lot of people who, at some point, looked in the mirror and said, "You're _______." (Fill in the blank with your own self-defeating assessment of you.) We all have those moments when we bully ourselves.

I'm not suggesting we turn into affirmation robots, but it's time to muzzle our internal critics. In writing this, I realized I never go to bed thinking about some stupid something someone else said or did. I only critique myself. Logically, that's probably true for others. I can assume that no one else is giving a second thought to the stupid thing I said at dinner. In truth, half the people weren't really listening to me; they had their own squirrels running around in their heads.

I am my biggest obstacle.

I am my harshest critic.

Criticism is good if you learn from it. But if, in the process, you just break your own heart, then that's a bad habit to break.

Hopefully, this book puts you in sync with who you are in your life and where you want to go in the near future. If you stop breaking your own heart, perhaps this will be your final investment in self-improvement.

"ARE YOU AN EX-SOMETHING, OR ARE YOU YOUR NEXT SOMETHING?"

I said this to myself one day as if the yogi within suddenly found his voice.

Two days prior, I'd finished a class and had a coffee with a few fellow yogis. I barely knew them, so it was a lot of getting-to-know-you chatter.

I find that when meeting people at this grayhead stage in life, many people want me to know who they were—before they moved out of the city, before they retired, before they were divorced…before now.

I can sense it—they felt more vital, valuable, and interesting in their pasts. They were quite fond of their ex-self. That's not a bad thing, unless they also wished they were *living* in the past.

You are not who you were.

You are who you are right now.

The people you meet today will never share your past. To connect with life today, we need to keep writing our story.

My friend Laura in Santa Fe has thrown herself into a painting collective. The focus is portraiture. It's clearly evident: She was a painter in a previous life. In her portraits, the soul of the subject radiates from the center of each canvas. Laura's identity shifted overnight. Just three years ago, she was an advertising creative director. The people who meet her now meet an artist. In fact, they meet an exceptional artist, which begs the question: "Laura, why did you spend twenty-five years in advertising?"

Laura is now effortlessly happy.

She's exactly where she wants to be.

She's not an ex-something. She's her next something.

I googled, "Why do people fear change?"

Google told me: "We fear change because the outcomes are unknown. Our brains are designed to find peace in knowing. When we don't know what will happen, we make up scenarios and, in turn, create worry. Humans find it hard to move on when something known comes to an end."

Fear of the unknown is a formidable enemy.

Since our early days on two feet, we worried about what was around the bend, hiding in the bushes or coming over the horizon. Predators take many forms; evil spirits, angry gods, and hostile invaders kept us on our knees in prayer. Lions, tigers, and bears are always out to get us. It is in our DNA to proceed with caution.

Whether you're forced into a significant change personally or professionally, don't think about what you're leaving behind.

Don't spend time being what you're not.

Hollywood is littered with has-beens—people who got stuck in who they were. Has-beens present an age-inappropriate image, a desperate attempt to hold on to that defining moment from thirty years ago. They were the promising young things, the breakthrough talent, the glowing ingenues and dreamy-eyed studs. Every year, there's a new it-list and A-list. The industry is desperate to crown the next Julia Roberts. Every two years, there's a coronation of this generation's James Dean. The movie industry was built on the kings and queens of ka-ching. Smoldering good looks always excite the business. But there's not much work for the wrinkly, bloated, dry-aged action star with oddly colored hair.

Success and failure in Hollywood both demand answers to the question, "What's next?" How do you follow up a mammoth success? How do you dig yourself out of failure? What's next for you when you're too old to be the cute, hot, sexy, studly, or boffo-box-office version of you? Longevity is so rare. The A-list is short, and even that list gets culled every year. The Meryls and Toms are the unicorns in the business. That's why we love a comeback story; comebacks are our pop-cultural reassurance that even if our light has dimmed, our story isn't finished.

The people who find their way to long careers have to dig deep and take chances.

I put Jessica Lange in the Brand Reinvention Hall of Fame. Look at *Tootsie* and *Frances*; her ethereal beauty *almost* masked her talent as an actress. When you're that beautiful, the whole world notices when age begins to steal your youth. Sadly, in our culture, age can make you less rather than more of who you are. But not Jessica. She transformed into a commanding presence. Her talent said, "Don't look at me, watch me," and we've been treated to a gallery of complex and breathtaking characters. Today, we don't think of Jessica Lange as the girl trapped in King Kong's desire. Now, when Jessica enters a scene, she leaves the past behind. Jessica's power and appeal are rooted in her talent. Her allure isn't a reflection of who she was, it's fueled by who she is right now.

Knowing what's "now" is how you discover what's next.

"HE STARTED YOGA AT EIGHTY-FIVE?!"

I'm still new to yoga. Every teacher has something unique to offer that makes a difference in my practice. I check out another studio. There's only one familiar face in the room. We nod at each other as if we've been caught cheating on our favorite yogi. We were settling in with mats, blocks, and straps, looking out at a perfect day. There was a guy walking across the lawn, heading our way with a yoga mat rolled under one arm. I blurt out to no one specifically, "Is this guy coming to yoga?"

"Yep," the woman behind me answers.

"He's, like, a hundred?"

"Eighty-eight. Yeah—he started three years ago."

"He started yoga at eighty-five?!"

"Yep."

"No! Really?"

"His wife died.... She'd been sick...a long time. He did everything—the chores, the meds, the nursing—just to keep her at home."

Underneath the silence, I heard my heart break.

"Can he...actually...?"

"Yes. He moves slower than everyone, but he lands every pose."

There's more to this story. There's more to everyone's story. Over time, I got bits and pieces. He talked in bits and pieces.

He and his wife had been young and sparkly-eyed. Ocean swimmers—much more challenging than laps in a pool. No kids—but that was their choice. They were each other's everything. They didn't need anything else. They had an easy togetherness, accumulating buckets of happiness over sixty-seven years.

Gardening.

Puzzling over puzzles.

Inhaling books until their eyes cried for rest.

They didn't travel the world because they kept going back to the same place: Italy. Italy had everything they wanted in one place: history, art, music, mountains, and, of course, food. In Italy, they could also swim for hours in glorious shades of blue-and-green water.

There were eight inches of snow in the Dolomites when they were hiking at the end of June. Imagine, snow in June. Shorts in a snowstorm. That was a day.

One day, maybe ten years ago, his wife couldn't find the car keys. The freezer isn't the first place you look when your keys have gone missing, but that's where her keys were. They had a good laugh about it. It was a funny story to tell. "Senior moment" became a familiar refrain.

But then the television remote wound up in the oven.

Water left running in the kitchen.

Groceries left in the car overnight. Fifty-six dollars' worth of shrimp gone bad.

She sat quiet at a birthday dinner with friends. But she always was the quiet one, wasn't she? But he knew she wasn't just being quiet; she seemed lost. He looked into her eyes but couldn't see the woman he'd known all those years.

Then, long silences. "Nothing to say?" answered with a smile.

Then there was the call to police:

"Our Volvo's been stolen. From the parking lot."

"Where, ma'am?"

"Here. It was right here. In the parking lot."

"Where, ma'am? What parking lot?"

She can't find her answer.

"What parking lot, ma'am?"

"Groceries…"

"IGA?"

"No. The other one."

"Stop & Shop?"

The Volvo was home; she'd forgotten that she'd driven the truck that day. She'd planned to stop by the nursery for spring plantings.

The decline accelerated into a steady and determined downward spiral. He devoted years to watching over her every waking moment. He attended to her every need.

Diminished strength.

Shaky hands. A drink of water required a sippy cup.

The creeping loss of his one true everything blanketed their last five years together. Every day, he woke up to a fog of mourning. Life became a cave of agony—a tug-of-war, hoping for the end while praying for a few more "good days." He waited to see that smile one more time—that smile they shared decades ago when they first recognized each other as their forever-and-evers.

Without warning, the moment came. Even if you know it's coming, you can't prepare for it. Your other half…gone.

The end. That final moment lingers in the room.

You want to rewind, even to just two minutes ago. To say, "My love," just one more time.

The survivor doesn't know how to take their next breath. They're suspended in a soundless vacuum. And yet the silence is deafening.

"What happens now…?"

There is a to-do list that comes with someone's passing.

There are rituals and calls with friends and family.

He remembers the day, staring at her toothbrush and wondering when or if he even could get rid of it.

"It's not something to keep, is it?"

That seems odd—keeping an old toothbrush—but not if this is your story. If you're ever him, hopefully, the day will come when you wake up ready to tackle the question for yourself.

"Now what?"

There's either going to be a "something next" or an even more painful nothing.

So this dude got up one day, got in the truck, and drove to a yoga studio.

The young woman at the front desk—she had the look and spirit of Kate Hudson in *Almost Famous*—met his mournful stare with her smiling eyes and wondered, "Hi, are you here to do yoga?"

"I heard yoga might be good for me."

"Yoga can be great for you."

And, so it began. The first day of the rest of his life. Even though it made me really nervous, the dude could do a headstand. For the record, I can't; I have an overdeveloped sixth sense of possible and probable injuries waiting for me in any and all inversion poses. But this guy, decades older than me, had nothing in his way. Maybe that's what happens when you get that old. You stop worrying about dying, because you don't want to waste any living you've got left.

That afternoon, I walked my dog, Cookie, on the beach. It was early November, but it felt like September. I thought about the old dude upside down in a headstand.

The muscles between my eyes relaxed. I felt a smile. It was a moment of emotional Botox; if I could have seen myself, I'm sure I didn't look a day over forty-nine.

I said to Cookie, "Hey, girl, look at this day! Just about everybody we know is stuck in some endless meeting, looking out the window and wondering where else they could be on this spectacular day."

I had a flash—an inkling about writing a book. Hmm…a new focus. New purpose. A desire to be creative again. Not a creative ideation about the uniqueness of a mascara brush or a heated debate about infinitesimal adjustments to a TV spot. For me, crafting ad copy was like playing with the pieces of a formulaic puzzle. It requires clever wordplay. "Creative" for me means conjuring something from nothing. I wanted to get back to that version of me that wrote plays, sketches, and scripts, wrestling with my imagination to craft something worthy of your attention. But in this moment, this flash about writing again was easy to ignore.

Every time I see the old dude, I remind myself that the answer to "now what?" is best answered in the right now. Age should never define us, limit us, or excuse us, and at a certain age, there is no long-term plan or consequences. It really is about right now. Surely, an upside down eighty-eight-year-old has to be the international symbol for "never too late."

Never too late for absolutely anything.

"YOUR BODY WILL NEVER DO WHAT IT DIDN'T LEARN TO DO THIRTY YEARS AGO."

That was a yogi being kind to me, reacting to my pouty face as I repeatedly fell short of achieving a bound triangle.

"It's because I have big thighs," I always tell myself when my fingertips strain to reach each other but fail to connect in a bind.

"Your body can't turn back the clock. It can make up for lost time, but it can't go back to change the future. You are where you are."

Translation: "It's not your thighs. It's you."

When I dove back into yoga, I was swimming with blind optimism. I was determined to bend and twist into the same beautiful and powerful shapes of the thirty-year-olds' bodies surrounding me. Classes were equal parts inspiration and frustration. I saw where I wanted to go physically, but my body wouldn't go there. I made progress, but I had many miles to travel before I'd catch up to Surf Jesus—a fellow yogi who seemed to arrive from yogi heaven. Tall, but not too tall. Built, but not self-consciously muscular. Longish hair, but not trashy. Like a guy who looked good with a guitar. Surf Jesus also had remarkably clean feet. After decades of running, I'd become acutely aware of my ugly feet. My husband refers to them as bear claws.

Every move he made was effortless. He was always fluid and flawless. He had a calm control over every build in a sequence while I teetered on the verge of a spastic collapse, my toes gripping the floor and begging for balance.

On the whole, most guys doing sun salutations don't look all that hot. Basketball. Volleyball. Speed skating. If the sport requires grunting—guys look hot. And quarterbacks. Quarterbacks are universally hot. Yoga guys—they can be lithe, light, sinewy, defined, or, oddly, even a little chubby. But they're not traditionally hot…at least in my mind.

Except for Surf Jesus. Effortlessly hot is the hottest of hots.

About a year into my practice, I was more agile, more limber, and stronger, but I was never going to be this guy. In him, I recognized the key ingredient of attractiveness: It's not just physical attributes, it's simply being at ease. If I could see myself in a mirror, I'd see a pained face contorted by my effort. It's like with a contestant on *American Idol*—you don't want to see them trying way too hard to hit the high notes. A person at ease is like a mermaid; you want to believe they exist but can't imagine how it's even possible.

My yoga teacher sensed my frustration, maybe because I finished each salutation with a sullen face. When we huddled after class one day, she stated the obvious: "Your body will never do what it didn't learn to do thirty years ago. You can get where you want to go, but it could take years to unlearn and unravel what your body has been through. You probably didn't run ten miles the first time you put on running shoes. You're starting here. Starting now. This is where you're at."

She'd given that speech before. I wasn't the only boomer who arrived at yoga after a lifetime of type-A workouts and thought they should immediately be able to kick butt in the yoga studio. And by that, I mean, "I should be able to do these stupid poses, no problem!"

Even though they may be fleeting, this was one of *those* moments: I wish I was twenty-eight again.

I want to have hair you want to touch.

I want a jawline that works with a turtleneck.

I want a waist.

I'd like to tuck my shirt into my pants knowing it's a good look for me.

But we are who we are. We are where we're at. The older you are, course correction becomes more of a challenge. Just try losing five pounds.

For most of my life, I could do that in a weekend. But, more recently, I haven't been able to lose five pounds over the last ten years. Acceptance isn't half the battle—it is the battle. If Cher and all her surgeons can't turn back time, neither can we.

I already had this wisdom inside me, but it was packed away in the back of my mind. Looking good for your age is not the same as erasing time.

You can't be what you're not.

It was 1991. I'm thirty-five. Still youngish in NY but a very awkward age in LA. I was in a gay bar on Santa Monica Boulevard. I wasn't shopping. I had just moved to town, and a new friend was giving me a Friday-night tour of WeHo. In a dimly lit corner of Motherlode was a man probably twenty years my senior, working all he had to his best advantage. He definitely got an A for effort. Good hair. Good face. In shape, and by that, I mean his shirt was tucked into his jeans. But he looked slightly uncomfortable. But standing alone in a corner of a gay bar isn't really a comfortable thing for most people.

I was brimming with new-in-town friendliness, which, sadly, dissipates in about three months. We signaled him to join us at the bar. Out of the dark, he teetered our way. And by "teetered," I mean walking like he was wearing a too-tight pencil skirt. In the light, the fatal flaw was revealed. Cowboy boots. A vain attempt to be a little taller and a bit more butch than he was. The moment gave me one of my steadfast fashion mandates: If you didn't grow up wearing cowboy boots, don't start now.

You'll never be what you're not. You'll never be who you never were. No point in lamenting, regretting, or resenting your truth. You're here. Be the amazing you you are right now.

Wow, Michael, that's very Marianne Williamson of you.

But we all need a little bit of Marianne, don't we? She didn't just happen. She is what people were looking for—Marianne was self-care before self-care was invented.

Marianne might ask, "Who can you become in the next year? Looking ahead three years—or five years—don't think about what you want or what you need. Don't set goals. Think about how you want to feel in your life."

For most people, if you didn't grow up walking on real dirt, cowboy boots just aren't who you are. They might make you taller, but you'll always be walking a little funny.

There it is, just what the yogi said: "Your body is never going to do what it didn't learn to do thirty years ago."

Be here now.

"DO NOT LAMENT THE THINGS YOU CAN'T CONTROL."

I devour these bits of inspiration as if they're yogi fortune cookies. I like them. Easily digestible. Skip the deep analysis and just boil it down to the key truths and insights. When you get to the essence of anything, the unencumbered truth unveils a deep and compelling story.

When Labor Day hits the Hamptons, there is a sulky farewell to summer. It's a familiar pain we learned as kids when September required our return to the confines of school. But we're not eleven, and there's nothing to be done but celebrate the invigorating energy that accompanies fall's arrival.

When something ends, it's over.

Life is marked by endings: high school, college, relationships, vacations, holidays, jobs—even your "greatest TV show ever" eventually comes to an end.

Loss is inevitable. Parents, pets, friends—even a good head of hair—take their leave. We can't control how, when, or why we'll be required to absorb the pain of saying goodbye. We can't always flip the switch and move on. Ultimately, we must accept a destiny not of our own design. Sure, you can replace the collagen your body stops producing, but do you really want to become a Smurf-face?

In yoga, body type is destiny. The same can be said about pants. I've got Bonobos thighs and a Brooks Brothers butt. I was not made for

Levi's 501s. But now, in my desperate search for pants that fit, when I stand in front of a dressing room mirror, I have the calming voice of a yogi in my head: *Do not lament the things you can't control.*

In life, this means people too. Friends, bosses, lovers—many of them disappoint us in different ways. Some things just are and need to be left in the past.

Caveat: If your entire life is wiped out by a raging fire, calamitous storm, or random violence, you get a hall pass. If you happen to be in the wrong place at the wrong time, you have every right to be pissed. Like, Tonya Harding pissed. Tonya was a force of nature—that girl could jump—but she was never going to be Nancy Kerrigan. Nancy had the grace and face of a champion. Tonya was never the all-American blonde she hoped she could be. Nancy had surf Jesus' ease; Tonya was like me when I try to do a bind, you could see how hard she was trying. Accept who you are, and you'll have one less battle to fight.

I just realized skating is at the root of many of my metaphors. I am not a skater. Not in this life. Not with my Brooks Brothers butt. But I will not lament the things I can't control.

Next life.

I'm sure I'll have a quad jump in me by then.

"BE A BEGINNER."

INT. YOGA STUDIO, a crisp November evening.

Class starts as a full moon takes ownership of the darkening sky.

YOGI: …Chaturanga Dandasana, and we all wind up in downward dog for three breaths.

During those breaths, I feel good. Strong. My feet don't flatten out onto the floor like other yogis, but they never will.

YOGI: Right leg up and back. Now, knee to nose….

I know where we're going. I shoot my leg through and lift myself into a high lunge.

YOGI: Don't get ahead of me. Don't get ahead of yourself. In fact, today, let's all be beginners.

ME: Oh god, another philosophy. Does everyone know it's me? Again, I'm the problem.

YOGI: Heading into the new year, that's a really good mindset. Reset—right? That's what we do in January. Come to class like a

> beginner. Ready to listen. Ready to follow. Ready to learn. If this class becomes routine for you, then we're both not doing the job we're supposed to do on the mat today. Let's take that right leg back and up. Now, knee to nose....

Class went on from there. I moved with the eyes and ears of a beginner.

I was always a beat behind the instruction but always on point with the moves I needed to make. Instead of mindless flow, my salutations were defined by the nervous concentration of a beginner. The focus gave me clear and exact intention. There was an exactitude in my execution. I assumed nothing.

It's like when you travel. You're drawn to the details of a place the locals no longer see. Nothing is routine or unseen. The early days of your career are similarly exhilarating; your fresh eyes add a valuable perspective because they aren't blinded by assumption or experience. And nothing beats the intense thrill of first love. As relationships evolve, it's easy to lose sight of the person with whom you fell in love.

Leaving class, the yogi gave me a "caught you" smile.

"You did. You caught me...."

"Yeah—you weren't doing yoga. You were doing a routine."

"I got it. Be a beginner. In everything you do."

With a one-eyebrow arch, she underscores the point: "Everything is better if it feels new."

I think to myself, *Hmm. That one has an amazing sex life.*

"EVEN FLOWERS KNOW TO TURN TO THE LIGHT."

I'm not the only person who sometimes (okay—maybe too often) wants what I can't have. I'm not just talking stuff. I want life to *feel* like that song that becomes *the* song of the summer. I want that blast of pop energy we got every time we heard the first chords of "Flowers" or "About Damn Time."

But that's not the way my life plays. I've always walked in heavy shoes.

I want to be as popular as everyone else seems to be. I can't be the only one who thinks there's another version of this life I may have missed. Often, my work helps me answer my personal questions.

I conducted a qualitative research study on the divorce journey in 2016. Talking mostly with women in the process of ending their marriage, there were a few very sad facts:

- An overwhelming majority of these women remain silent about their unhappiness for more than three years.
- When they first use the word "divorce," it's only voiced in an internal monologue. "Divorce" gets mulled around in the head for an average of eighteen months before it is even whispered to a friend or family member.
- One woman told me that in her twenty years of marriage, she and her husband rarely spoke at the dinner table. Every night, the family came together for the evening meal, but for the most

part, they ate without speaking a word. No conversation. No sharing their day. No jokes. No joy. Sharing her story, she confessed, "We could hear each other chew," conjuring a scene in my mind you might see in a David Lynch film:

INT. KITCHEN – A WINTER EVENING

The quiet is extreme. There is a dark world outside the windows of this home. The cold of Colorado seems to keep everything on ice. A husband and wife—their faces are hungry for sleep—finish up the last bites of a chicken dinner. Their two preteen boys lack the usual animation of happy children. Tommy, the younger boy, seems unaware of his foot shaking under the table.

CLOSE ON TOMMY, wanting so much to find something to say. His desire is painful, but like a dog with a bark collar, he knows not to speak.

The adults keep their eyes focused on their plates, as if the movement of their utensils must be carefully monitored.

THE WIFE'S POV, her eyes begin to lift, traveling across the table. She takes in the plaid of her husband's shirt. She then sees the flesh of his neck. His clean-shaven jawline stops chewing. Quickly, her eyes return to her plate.

THE CAMERA PULLS BACK, out through windows and pulling away from the house, revealing a generic split-level in the midst of many others, each with a family attending to the rituals of dinner time with joyful togetherness.

SFX: A cold wind screeches through the night.

SCENE.

Back to reality. Back to the woman who inspired that scene. Their remote relationship was never questioned; it was their normal. Both husband and wife were emulating what they experienced around their childhood dinner tables. Silence. In a twisted way—they were a perfect couple. They had each inherited a tolerance for devastating loneliness.

I'm all for working through problems. I'm a big fan of talking it out. Communication can shine a bright light on misunderstandings. But not every frown is a smile turned upside down. If you're sitting silent about something in your life, chances are you're screaming about it inside your own head. How do we break the rules and expectations that bully your brain?

Instincts. Our instincts point us to our light.

Instincts come with their own light source. It takes practice to even hear what you might instinctively know. Instincts are easy to ignore because they often point in a direction we don't want to go.

We stretch. Hydrate. Workout. All with the intent of looking good and feeling great. Let's treat our emotional responses like muscles. We want our responses and reactions to be flexible, healthy, and strong. When staring down the shit that life throws your way, find the energizing spirit in life. Don't let the negative overwhelm, consume, or define your day. Turn to the light. It's what nature wants us to do.

When a friend disappoints me, I bleed. I would pick at that wound and make it worse. It wasn't easy, but I found a new practice. Now, I simply pick up the phone and call another friend. Someone who makes me laugh. A friend that feels like a solid connection. A dialogue that's clear, unencumbered, and effortless.

"Bone marrow friend" is a criteria my beautifully intelligent friend Simone uses to determine who she invites to take up residence in her psyche: "Bone marrow friends are there for you no matter what, no matter when. Name the people you'd ask to pick you up from your colonoscopy. They're your real friends. Everyone else—companions."

You want to keep company with your natural "fits"—the people, places, jobs, and relationships where you naturally shine.

Lean toward them. In their light, you stand tall.

"YOU CAN'T THINK YOUR WAY OUT OF IT."

Well, that's fucking nonsense! I thought.

As if she heard me, the yogi continued, "You can't tell your body what to do, it has to work it out for itself."

Thinking is what I do for a living!

"Thinking can get in the way of doing," she said, apparently reading my mind.

Really?! Do you watch the news? People need to spend more time thinking before they say and do really dumbass things.

I wouldn't say I overthink everything; I'd say I'm hypervigilant in my thought process. This yogi's farmhouse philosophy is minimizing the value of my greatest muscle: the ability to think my way out of strategic binds. Thinking through brand positions, creative platforms, copy assignments, story structure, script dialogue. In marketing, you get paid for "the doing"—the deliverables—but there's a lot of thinking that precedes "the doing."

"Thinking" through the emotional contortions of life is also what makes me a good friend. I've often played amateur therapist. I have a good ear. Growing up gay in a closeted world, "listening" was a tactic employed to deflect the conversation away from myself. As I shared earlier in this book, I put in the ten thousand hours as a GBF; I'm quite adept at directing personal and professional relationships over and around the speed bumps of life's confusion and disappointment.

Don't react. Think.

Ask a follow-up question.

Think again, then respond.

Thinking is a way of being in the world. It creates the calm instead of the storm.

My mind came back to the room. The more advanced yogis in the class were in a pose I couldn't even attempt. I reminded myself, *My flexibility is compromised because I have big thighs.*

You now see, thighs are my usual explanation for everything impossible.

"You can't think your way out of a pose."

She then added insult to the insult: "And I'm not just talking yoga poses!"

There was a slight trace of indignance that etched its way across the Fraxeled faces of her devoted followers.

As with almost everything, those tidbits pierced my psyche.

How dare you?! I scream inside my head with a full-on Glenn Close/ *Fatal Attraction* wild-eyed resentment.

"I see I've confused you," she said, preparing to share one of her greatest hits. "Sometimes you can't think it out—you just have to live it out."

Yep, there it was—a yoga teacher reaching for a catch phrase. Three little words that say it all. "Live it out" was begging to be a T-shirt. A coffee mug. A theme for a week-long retreat in Tulum.

What if she's right? She is smart about a lot of things. In fact, she's like a Swiss Army knife of practical knowledge.

I can't quote a lot of movies, but in *Notes on a Scandal*, when a twisted Judi Dench commanded a cowering Cate Blanchett to just "do do do," Cate and I were equally terrorized. Certainly, Sheba, Cate's character, had no business shagging a fifteen year old boy. Barbara, Judi's obsessive and possessive character, knew that too much thinking can overcomplicate this messy situation. Sometimes, the "doing" informs how you think through a problem. In the world according to Barbara, this troublesome relationship just has to die. Right now! So, in a very British way, get on with it then.

Do do do! I guess it's like that with poses?

It's difficult for me to break the reliance on disaster-checking every decision. As soon as I make a restaurant reservation, I make another. A backup. One on OpenTable. The other on Resy. A just-in-case backup option without really knowing why I might need the second option.

It's never easy for me to decide on a hotel, which is such a waste of time since all that really matters is that there's decent coffee in the neighborhood.

Which flight should I book? What books do I pack for a trip? What Netflix series should I start watching now?

Should I buy the irregularly shaped pasta bowls or are they stupid?

These are sand traps, silly time sucks that get me nowhere. Overthinking assumes that there's a perfect answer. There is no perfect restaurant; it's the mix of friends around the table that truly matters.

Sometimes, you see the solution in the rearview mirror as you move forward. You may need to leave before you figure out where you want to go. Maybe you need to quit before you know what you want to do. Big decisions can paralyze you, but staying in the status quo can be like making a left turn into gridlock. You'll get nowhere fast.

Like a complicated yoga pose, we get ourselves into situations that have no graceful exit. The tools of reason—logic, perspective, and experience—don't always provide the answer. Sometimes, you have to feel your way forward.

Wouldn't it be amazing if we had Waze for our personal journeys?

Delays ahead. Exit left and find a new career.

At the light, turn right, wait two months and meet someone new.

Found a better route to a happier place. Exit now.

It's what I learned in yoga. You can't think your way through a pose, you just have to "do" it and move through it. The body knows more than the brain.

A pivot doesn't mark a mistake. It's often prompted by an insight. But sometimes you don't know what's good for you until you move though it.

"IF YOU FEEL OVERWHELMED, JUST DO THE NEXT RIGHT THING."

The pursuit of perfect makes sense for Olympians, but the rest of us are not being scored by an international federation of judges. The best career move? The best place to stay? Who has the best coffee?

There is a new addiction: best-aholism. It's the compulsion to research, analyze, and explore every option for every decision, made possible by the devil itself: Google. I've been trapped online till 1:30 a.m. in search of the perfect vacuum. I spent over two hours comparing tamarind chutneys thanks to the rabbit hole of "search." I am stuck in an endless quest to find the pants that will make nice with my hefty thighs. Yes—I want my pants, vacuums, and chutneys to be the best they can be, as long as the pursuit of the best isn't a frustrating time suck that interrupts my pursuit of a solid night's sleep.

I spent an hour last night deciding what to watch next on my ever-expanding list of streaming options. This is the list of shows and movies friends have insisted with a dash of condescension, "You have to watch! I can't imagine you won't love it." They are the shows that never make it to the top of the list, but they remain on the list, taunting the culture vulture that lives inside me:

Compartment No. 6
The Fall
Denzel's *Macbeth*

Test Pattern
The Bridge (Danish)
Shtisel
The Bureau
Lovecraft County
Wandavision
The Mandalorian
All Creatures Great and Small
Gomorrah
Tehran
The Boys

I also need to finish *A French Village* (tuned out when it turned into a soap opera), *Yellowstone* (one season would have been great), *The Restaurant*, *Abbott Elementary* (I'm either too old or not old enough for sitcoms), *The First Lady* (never clicked with it), *A Very British Scandal* and *Anatomy of a Scandal* (I forget the difference between those two series), *Rita* (what's awesome becomes repetitive), *Bergen* or *Borgen* or whatever that show is, and *The Plot Against America* (too close to reality). I also admit to dropping out of *Better Call Saul* after two episodes, which makes no sense since *Breaking Bad* is the most exhilarating experience I've ever had in my living room.

Since I seem to be the odd man out with my peers, I suppose, at some point, I need to give *Succession* and *The Wire* a second try.

Lists! They organize and frustrate you in equal measure.

How do we avoid the paralysis of overwhelming options?

When we get to the intersection of "what if?" and "what now?", we don't always know where to turn.

When you want to make a move, think about it, but not too long. Critical information is always waiting for us in what lies ahead, which you can't access by staying where you are.

Forward motion trumps paralysis. When you don't know what to do or where to go, don't try to figure out the "best" or "most" choice. Whenever you're unsure which move is the winning move, just make a good move.

There are shows I resisted in spite of passionate recommendations. I had zero interest in *Breaking Bad*, *My Brilliant Friend*, *Kimi*, *Babylon Berlin*, *The Other Two*, *Barry*, *Generation War*, *American Crime Story*, *Homeland*, *Schitt's Creek*, or *Catastrophe*. Succumbing to the insistent chorus of "You must!" and "You will love it!", I pressed play on episode one of each of those series. Five minutes in, all of these shows immediately became lovefests.

We are overwhelmed by options. The too-muchness of our media landscape and consumer marketplace is blunting our ability to make decisions.

Here's a snippet from one of my lectures at Parsons:

THERE IS NO RIGHT ANSWER.

LECTURE VOICEOVER:

"With every strategic and creative challenge, you can probably find at least three good solutions. They might be similar or wildly different, but each has value in its distinctive possibilities. How do you decide? Assess which one is *feasible* (within the confines of budget, timing, and team), and which one is the most *fun* (for you, your teams, your client, and the consumer). Pick one and fall in love with it."

That same criteria can be applied to almost every decision you face. Always check the box next to "first, do no harm" and then relax; a good move is your next best move. At the very least, it's better than no move at all.

In Scrabble, even if your move sucks, just make a move, unless you have five vowels and two one-point letters. If you can't lay down at least four letters and get ten points, your best move is to turn your letters in and grab new tiles. In Scrabble, when you're overwhelmed by vowels, taking a pass is the next best thing to do...and that's always a good way to go.

Students are always looking for the correct answer. They want the A. There is no answer key to most of the decisions we have to make in life. Reviews. Likes. Ratings. We rely so much on the data at our fingertips that we've forgotten how to listen to our gut. In life, "instinct" has the value of a seven-letter word in Scrabble.

"WHEN YOU WANT POWER, YOU HAVE NONE."

Beauty. Money. Youth.

These are three reliable sources of personal power.

Youth, beauty, and money can easily seduce people who are void in those suits.

In their presence, terra firma dissolves into quicksand.

Of course, all three are relative and subjective.

It's not surprising that a class in Tribeca would commence with a more transactional meditation. People don't move to New York to relax. The city is not a place you can just wing it. People arrive here, ready to trade on what they have in order to *become* whatever they're not. It's not a bad thing. NYC is the intersection of survival and ambition.

Beauty comes in many forms and always lives in the eye of the beholder. But one thing is standard: People who are perceived to be beautiful enter a room with an enviable ease. Experience has taught them to anticipate a welcoming world. They are products of a world that gives them preference on a daily basis. Without even trying, their mere presence always feeds someone's desire.

We spend significant time, money, and energy trying to look good:

- Cosmetic procedures: $50B in the US
- Beauty industry: $500B globally
- Fitness industry: $32B in the US

It's obvious that most people wish their mirror told another story.

Conversely, there's nothing more intoxicating than the person who makes us feel beautiful. Alluring. Or fuckable.

We pour hard-earned money into the fragrance industry, metatarsal-crunching heels, body waxing, and CoolSculpting. Even hot people want to be hotter than they are.

We have made beauty a sport. From state fairs to the national stage, beauty pageants have crowned "the fairest of them all" for hundreds of years. Bodybuilding competitions, hot firemen calendars, and Mr. Leather contests provide grown men with the same opportunity to compete in the context of a collective standard of hotness.

Beautiful people aren't the enemy. We give beauty the power that it holds over us. With their Campaign for Real Beauty, Dove goes to war against the tyranny of the beauty industry, celebrating the beauty of women in all shapes, sizes, ages, and skin tones. Since the campaign launched in 2004, they've been consistent and persistent in their messaging. The imagery is carefully crafted to liberate women from judging themselves against the airbrushed, impossible standards of beauty. Empowering women with an ironclad sense of self-esteem is, in itself, a beautiful thing.

Really? Then why is Instagram jammed with people who use every lighting trick and digital filter to show their world just how cute, perfect, gorgeous, and fabulous they are?

Instagram is the boxing ring for beautiful people, all vying for your eyeballs. They use their looks to tease their way into your life. That daily feed of smiles, curves, and muscle is their money machine. Or so they hope. Instagram is living proof that no matter how much our consciousness is raised, beauty is a drug. It's our primal attraction to whatever makes us go weak in the knees. And if you've ever been an object of desire, you've tasted the power you can wield. But beauty has its own weakness—the steadfast march of time.

"Youth is wasted on the young."

George Bernard Shaw's famous quote makes very little sense until your body starts acting its age. Had Shaw been a yoga teacher, he surely would have opened his classes with some very dramatic bits of inspiration. Forget the "young at heart" and "you're as old as you feel" bullshit. Yoga isn't the fountain of youth—but you'd look and feel older without it.

Uncompromised energy is the plus-one of youth. Rarely do we realize the power of youth while we're still young. We don't see it until it starts to slip away. Youthful energy gets buried by the realities and responsibilities of the life you build. Mortgages. Kids. Careers. They are the thieves that steal the breezy exuberance of youth.

The fearlessness of youth can be a disturbing rattle in the midst of a mature audience. Perhaps it's the table next to you in a restaurant or a random conversation with a "newbie" at a sales convention; you see the difference in your composed energy juxtaposed with their unedited spirit. You can't help but feel a tad envious. You shudder at the thought, *I'm not who I used to be.*

Weirdly, at forty, you can feel old and young, depending on your context. It's the second time in life you're a "tween." When you're twelve, you seesaw between the safety of being a kid and the urge to wear the independent bravura of teenager. At forty, you're a "tween" again: Your spirit clings to your spontaneous past as it flirts with the confident joy of a downshift. If you live well, you can look and feel ten years better than your peers. By my calculation, I look ten years older after a Manchego cheese binge and two too many martinis.

But forty is also the age of disbelief. You won't believe how old you look in a photo taken next to a twenty-eight-year-old at a cocktail party or family gathering. It's worse if it's a summer party. Following the dire warnings of your dermatologist to avoid the sun, there you are—pasty and pale—posing with a twenty-eight-year-old in her gauzy, flowy, sky-blue halter-top dress, revealing even more of her tight, sun-drenched skin.

When we look in the mirror, do we see ourselves naturally maturing or do we see our youth disappearing? It's only when we start aging that we recognize the power we had just being young.

Each week, when I get online to teach my class at Parsons, I am surrounded by eighteen Zoom squares of twenty-year-old faces. They are facing a much darker world than I was at their age, but still, their inquisitive spark is a powerful reminder that youthful energy is attractive at any age. No matter how much you try, you can't reclaim the face of youth, but you can reclaim the buoyancy of youth. And that will make people wonder, "What did they have done?"

Youth is fleeting. Beauty is determined by the genetic lottery. So maybe, just maybe, you have the power of money. Lucky you!

The allure of money can also be felt in the status that comes with a power position, a creative accomplishment, or the magnetic pull of fame. Granted, there's always somebody with more and somebody with less. I feel really rich in the subway and really poor in Hermès. When people have money, they have a confidence and calm that is undeniably attractive. They get to live what other people dream. People with money get to say yes more than they have to say no. And that's just fun. "Yes" doesn't just buy you stuff: It buys you experiences. It buys you access. It lifts you to a level above compromise. With money, you get stories to tell. There is no wasted time. There is no drudgery. There is no shopping for the best deal. The cheapest flight. You're not standing in line at a sample sale.

With money, there is security. You don't lose sleep because you're worried about the bills. You don't stress getting to the train on time. But you can still lose sleep if you open a second bottle of wine because now, sugar and carbs conspire to wake you up at 2:00 a.m.

The win comes when you want for nothing. That doesn't mean you're rich. It just means you're good with where you're at. And that's a powerful feeling.

If you always need more, you need to fix that sinkhole in your psyche.

If you're always looking to establish power, then you're juggling the demons of inferiority.

If you always want something bigger or better, you'll always appear smaller.

Never forfeit your power to the desire for stuff. A constant state of wanting is a constant state of stress.

Don't get me wrong, stuff is fun as long as it's just that—fun. But we know now that if we all want less, the planet will be happier.

Youth. Beauty. Money.

They are the power cards in the game of life.

If you crave youth…

If you are crippled by your imperfections…

If you never have enough…

If you feel less-than and always want more, you will always be weak.

Every insecurity I had was magnified when I moved to New York.

New York was the capital of success and excess.

The crazies came here to be their craziest.

Dreamers came to dream beyond their limits.

Beauty arrived dressed to kill.

Gays came to be gayer.

Ambition never had to apologize.

Addicts had lots of company.

Talent demanded to be seen and heard.

I arrived in town but forgot to pack enough crazy, edge, revenge, or ambition. I gave others power over my dreams. I was always in the mix, but I never stood out.

I never looked in the mirror and saw talent, ambition, or beauty.

I always hated looking at pictures of myself; I never saw who I was or who I might become, I only saw what I wasn't. It's telling—there isn't a single image of me smiling. I heard it a thousand times: "Oh my god, Norton, could you smile once?!"

Never. I wore the mask of steely confidence.

There's a picture of me taken in 1984, smoking a cigarette while stretched out in a bathtub at the Morgans Hotel. Ironically, today, I'd never allow myself to be photographed next to that twenty-eight-year-old me. In that picture, I had more power than I could see. Looking back at me then, I still see the me that felt powerless, old, ordinary, and poor. I was crippled by the fear of possibly never finding the path to my dreams. I know what I felt behind the façade. In that picture, I can see that the desperate desire for validation is never pretty.

I wish I knew then what I know now.

Maybe I'll know it all in my next life?

George Bernard Shaw also said, "Life isn't about finding yourself. Life is about creating yourself."

George definitely practiced some sort of yoga.

"CALM IS THE NEW POWER."

I think to myself, *Well, that's a yoga T-shirt if ever there was one.*

I'm at a hotel in Dallas. I may be the only guest who isn't part of a cult-like, Disney-produced national meeting for some insurance-related association. I join a yoga class in a hotel conference room. I'm the only one without a gold and blue water bottle. If anyone asks, I'll just say, "I'm the new guy."

Yogi has spikey hair and the vibe of Soul Cycle instructor. If this were the '90s, he'd be a high-kicking aerobics instructor. This will be a motivational yoga class, inspiration for hitting KPIs and "exceeding expectations" in year-end reviews.

"Yoga doesn't begin at the start of class. Yoga starts the minute you leave class."

I know where he's going. That's the value and the curse of practicing for a few years. You've learned enough to know better, but maybe not enough to live better. Maybe it's still just a class.

"Class ends with shavasana. Corpse pose. Still. Meditative. Restorative. How long does that feeling last?"

A realization: *I do love shavasana....*

Yogi downshifts into a soft voice, "Will you leave this room and immediately dive into your phone? Will your to-do list pull you back into the business of life? Will you curse the slow elevators...?"

The room twitters with forced, communal recognition.

My mind careens back into reality. I'm flying home today.

Gotta get the shirts still sitting at the dry cleaners. Remember to pick up Prilosec for the dog. Oh fuck—I have two more days to get the car inspected; the lines will be stupid.

"Imagine all of that 'stuff' but somehow holding on to the calm that comes with shavasana."

Yogi is so right. Just outside your door, there's a stressed-out, conflicted, anxious world waiting to freak you out. We navigate the day in defense mode. The mental wellness business is estimated to be more than $130 billion. Billion! The spa sector, workplace wellness, hot/mineral springs, and global wellness tourism grabs another $587 billion out of our collective pockets.

In 2017, the meditation market in the US was estimated to be worth around $1.21 billion and was predicted to grow to over $2 billion by the year 2022.

Mantras are big business!

Calm is that increasingly rare commodity that people pay dearly for. It's the gold rush of our time.

There are phone apps designed to relax your mind, coach you through your dramas, and help you cope, which is ironic given the increasing stress attached to the compulsive and disruptive relationship people have with their phones.

All of this signals an increased need to calm the squirrels running inside our heads.

Living in the golden age of outrage, a sense of calm is a true luxury. A stress-free moment is a treasure—a rarity—in our over-connected, over-hyped, overstimulated, over-sharing, over-opinionated world.

Yogi offers up a you-can-do-it big finish.

"When you feel good in your body, your energy feels young.

"When you see your reflection and see a person at ease, you love the way you look.

"When you have a response rather than a reaction, conversation can inspire possibilities.

"Got it? Calm is a superpower."

On that I agree, even if this yogi's presentation style seemed to be inspired by a familiarity with "Up with People" videos.

"BE BATTLE READY."

Everyone around me is seated cross-legged with hands in prayer position. Summer is on the horizon. Crowds descend on the roads, restaurants, and even yoga classes. Just stopping by the grocery store becomes a strategically planned chore. We're reminded that measured breathing is our secret weapon when navigating the hyped-up energy of summer.

The creative director in my head takes command of an imaginary staff meeting.

Be battle ready. Great tagline. Could be an Equinox campaign. I love the edge it would bring to cosmetics. It works with mouthwash, GNC, protein bars. Dunkin'. An IBS drug. Somewhere in the agency there's a client who could run with this. This is huge.

ME to me: I hate it when I talk in advertising cliches. That's not you anymore, anyway.

I'm now the only one who hasn't shifted into cat/cow.

ME reprimanding me: Get back in the room. Let's face it, no matter how centered you are on your mat, you'll leave here and cross paths with someone who is mad at the world.

ME coaching me: Focus!

Anything that can help us take on the world has value. The bits of wisdom that come with yoga equip us to fight the fights we stage inside our psyches. They position you to live more powerfully in your world:

balanced, focused, agile, spirited, and strong. That fortifies you to avoid, negotiate, or absorb the nonsense that comes your way.

According to the Yoga Alliance and *Yoga Journal*, about 15 percent of Americans have practiced yoga in the last six months. That leaves hundreds of millions of your fellow citizens ready to go to war with you over their right to talk in a movie theater or ride your bumper on I-95.

Why fight fire with fire? Maintaining calm is my weapon of choice.

Class ends.

I go directly to the cheese shop.

There's an imperious woman furious that they—these always joyful shopkeepers—have run out of her favorite rosemary crackers. The shopkeeper attempts to save the day,

"Oh no—over in the corner—in the basket—"

"No! The ones from England. The box—it's periwinkle." This customer has mastered the art of dismissive inflection.

This is the ruin of her weekend. The cheesemonger approaches with the necessary caution. "I can call and see if they have any in the Sag Harbor store…."

"And then what, I'm supposed to drive to Sag Harbor?"

An optimistic suggestion floats across the counter. "Lemon sea-salt crisps?"

Sounds like a tasty alternative to me.

The response is as sharp as the harshest cheddar. "The texture's not the same."

Her condescension is delivered as an act of violence, a way to extinguish the sunny disposition of the shopkeeper.

Every place has its assholes. The people who call the Hamptons "home" cherish their community. More often than not, our assholes are just visiting from the planet of self-entitlement. During the height of the summer, there is plenty of proof walking our streets that money doesn't buy happiness.

A snarly society will never be at peace. The Karens of the world should be sentenced to six months of Ashtanga yoga.

Yoga could be integrated into driver's ed, ensuring everyone behind the wheel has the tools to manage their road rage.

We could mandate that when we sing the national anthem, we must stand in tree pose with one hand over our heart.

Calm is the new power. Access to calm energy is a key ingredient in a sustainable world. It's not an alternative energy like wind or solar—it's a renewable energy whenever you meet your mat.

Eric Swalwell. Amy Klobuchar. Stacey Plaskett. Lisa Murkowski. Can one of you please draft legislation that requires every high school gym class to start and end with five minutes of yoga? Yoga should be a prerequisite for getting a high school diploma—proof that you can read, write, and think clearly.

"WHAT'S THE MOST INTERESTING THING ABOUT YOU?"

That question can be intrusive, provocative, inspiring, challenging, playful, or seductive. But really, it's mostly annoying.

It could be asked in a job interview. On a date. As an icebreaker at a business conference.

I was asked this question at the top of a yoga class.

"Breathe in to the count of six. Two, three, four, five, six. Breathe out to the count of six. Two, three, four, five, six. Repeat."

My thought bubble: *I hate breathing exercises.*

"Ask yourself, 'What's the most interesting thing about you?'"

No, let's not do this....

"Keep breathing. Find it. If you have an answer to it, hold it. Visualize it. Celebrate it. If you can't find it, keep that question with you throughout your practice today."

Don't tell me we'll come back to this at the end of class....

"Knowing what makes you beautifully unique gives you the power to grow into your true self. The same is true of our yoga practices. Your body is unique to you, and so is your practice. Yoga is not a competitive sport. It is a practice that serves you wherever your body can take you today."

WTF?

"*You* are where *you* are, but *we* are all here today."

She scores the "you" and "we" with big, sweeping hand motions that make me think of Cate Blanchett in *Tár.*

"*Every one of you* have come to your mat with the same intention. To be the best yogi *you* can be today."

I am *wildly relieved* we aren't going around the room to share our "most interesting thing...." But the question plays like an annoying polka twirling over and over in my head.

So much about me is quite ordinary. Cisgendered, slightly north of middle age, white guy, white hair that used to brown but sometimes gets a tinge of yellow because of the well water (or so I've been told). I've got brown eyes and, at my tallest, I'm 5′10.5″. That half inch is important to me. I have a lot of tall people in my life. I've always wanted to be 6′1″ or 6′2″—not too tall but with longer legs. I assume that with longer legs I'd be happier with the fit of my pants.

I'm smart but not brilliant.

Likeable, but my world doesn't revolve around me.

I'm successful enough, but I've often wished I'd had more ambition. Or is focus my problem? I spread myself thin; I want to taste everything that's new, and New York has a lot of new.

I've done some interesting things. Traveled more than the average person.

But there are lots of me in the world.

We're useful. We get the job done.

We can round out a dinner table.

We know lots of stuff. We're good guys to call when you want to know where to go or what to do.

But I haven't had a defining moment. No awards. No spectacular achievements. No shining moments.

But I do have spectacular dreams.

Vivid dreams cast with random but real celebrities.

My worst imaginary night—the most stressful—was my concert debut. I was backstage at a live, televised concert; it felt like an iHeartRadio holiday event. I was next up, and Carly Rae Jepsen was being so nice, trying to calm me down.

CARLY: Just sing your big hit.

ME: I don't have a big hit!

CARLY: Everybody here has at least one hit.

ME: Carly, I work in advertising.

CARLY: Oh—

ME: Yeah—oh!

CARLY: Then sing "Call Me Maybe."

ME: But that's your song.

CARLY: I'm good. I've got others. You'll be great.

And that was the end of that. Even after I woke up, I couldn't escape the nightmare. "Call Me Maybe" is way off-brand for me. It's too zippy. There is nothing about me that's zippy.

I enjoyed the dream when I was Eminem's date at the Grammy's. He won that night and basically came out to the world when he thanked me for being his inspiration. Aww!

Eminem is not gay.

I like him, but not like that. Eminem's not my type. "Not Afraid," "Love the Way You Lie," and, of course, "Lose Yourself" are on my playlist, but, in general, his music is not my music.

That said, in that insane night at the Grammy's, we were crazy, madly, and deeply in love. For some reason, Halle Berry was sitting next to me, but other than filling a seat, she played no role in the dream. It was just all about me and Eminem and an unforgettable night at Radio City Music Hall. I don't think I've ever been happier for another human being as I was for Eminem in that moment.

On another night, I was on *The Tonight Show*. Jay was the host. I had just won the gold medal for figure skating. At my age. The oldest gold medalist ever. America *loved* me. Even straight guys were replaying and reliving my triple-triple axel as if it were the winning play of a super tight Super Bowl. Leno teed up the clip of me spinning like a twister into a final, triumphant moment on the ice. Pandemonium in the arena. Teddy bears and flower bouquets rained down on the ice. Get this: A beaming Bruno Mars was in the stands, waving the flag! I skated to a mash-up of his hits.

I was a global sensation—the biggest story coming out of Vancouver in 2010.

And then I woke up. I was drowning in sadness as I swam toward the harsh light of reality. It took the greater part of that day to shake off the disappointment of just being me.

Not a champion.

Not a national treasure.

Not a magician on the ice.

Not even a good skater. It had been such a joyful moment; I desperately wanted to fall back into that fleeting moment of glory.

Our most vivid dreams happen during our REM cycles. In more than one REM cycle, Farrah Fawcett was my bestie and, oddly, I was still an undergraduate. She'd swing by Boston College so we could have a good catch-up. Her limo would pull up to the Eagle's Nest, an on-campus alternative to the dining hall, and Farrah—in full-on jumpsuit fabulousness—would sweep in and share a big chocolate frappé with me. I can't remember what we talked about. I'm not sure how we were friends. She was from Texas, and I was from New Jersey. Even though I was well past my twentieth reunion, I was still in college, and she was the most famous woman on the planet. Our only connection was that my hair had her same blown-out, feathery texture that inspired a billion haircuts in the 1970s. Anyway, she was always big hair, big smiles, and big hugs when I put her back in her limo. She'd roll down her window and wave at the openmouthed, dumbstruck students enroute to their next humanities class, many of whom had made sorry attempts to copy her look with a Conair blow dryer.

I learned not to question what these dreams signaled. They just happened. Sadly, I realized that I'm most interesting when I'm unconscious.

During the winter of our collective hibernation, on another night, my subconscious painted this little vignette: I was very busy collaborating with a makeup-free Rachel Maddow. I don't know what the project was, but our virtual collaboration was genius. In a musical montage, we worked magic with a Google doc.

Randall and I were prepping for Rachel and her wife to visit with us for the weekend.

Rachel texted, "GPS says 2:19 arrival."

Suddenly, after so many months of a social life powered by Zoom, I felt like we were possibly headed back to life as we knew it. Just before I woke up, Randall asked, "Do you think they'll play Rummikub?"

"I'm sure," I said. "But remember, we have to let guests win."

That's what hosts do.

Obviously, I've always been a little sad that Rachel was a no-show in real life.

A few years ago, sometime in the middle of the night, I won an Oscar for best documentary. I've never made a documentary. I've never had an idea for a documentary. I'm not even sure what my Oscar-winning documentary was even about. But there was something in the applause that told me it was a bit of a surprise win. My Oscar statue was waiting for me in the outstretched hands of Jodie Foster, who was wearing a pair of evening gloves.

Is Jodie a germaphobe? I wondered.

Jodie saw that I was terror-stricken. There were a billion eyeballs on me right then. She calmed me with a generously warm smile. There was a time when you didn't see Jodie smile—well, not as much as I wish she would have. As I reached for the statue, I realized, *Jodie's a nail biter, like me! Why else would she wear evening gloves in LA?* For the record, in recent years, Jodie smiles more. And it's a lovely smile.

I had an instant kinship with Jodie. Some of my best friends are nail biters. When she leaned in for the obligatory peck on the cheek, she whispered, "I voted for you."

I woke up in a restless state of confusion. Documentary? Outside of the specialized and dedicated community of documentary filmmakers, who dreams of winning an Oscar for documentary? I've written "real movie" scripts—why not best screenplay?

At least I got to meet Jodie Foster. Jodie's cool. In my files, I keep a copy of the article she wrote for *Esquire* magazine in 1982. It's a deeply personal account about the cost of fame. You can google it.

Truth be told—and I hope Jodie doesn't take offense—in my waking life, I've always thought that if I was ever racing to the podium to accept my Oscar, it would be fun to have big-hatted Diane Keaton announce my win. And I pray, like Jodie, Diane would lean in close and whisper, "La dee da. I voted for you."

I have a new recurring dream: There's me, vomitus and sweating, standing in the wings of a theater, waiting for my cue to make my entrance into a play I've never even read. Also, small detail, I'm not an actor.

Jude Law is perched in row seven, center seat. His sharp stare tells me everything I don't want to know: Jude Law had auditioned for my part, and he's here to enjoy my theatrical debacle. Who is the director who gave me this part over Jude Law? I saw Jude Law's Broadway debut in 1995. The play was *Indiscretions*. He was, as they say, a revelation. A force of nature.

On another night, in another dream, I'm across the pond, making my debut in the West End. The audience applauds my entrance. They seem to know me, as if I'd been in the cast of *Friends* or *The West Wing*. Oh god—I face the steely glare of my costar, Helen Mirren. Dame Helen knows I don't have a clue what my line is. In fact, again, I don't even know what play I'm in. She, along with all the other actors on stage, are costumed in Tudor drag. I have on white jeans, an old *Endless Summer* t-shirt that I love and James Perse sneakers.

I'm grateful every day that dreams can't wind up on YouTube. Nobody needs to see me bopping around like Carly Rae or vomiting at the feet of Helen Mirren. I suspect that Carly Rae is just as nice in real life. I also assume that Helen Mirren would have persevered, a true believer that the show must go on.

As for Jude Law, well, I can't say. In the dream, he didn't stick around for the curtain call and never came backstage. An unnecessary snub, even in the nether-regions of my subconscious. Yes—it was only a dream, but I still can't believe I got the part over him. My audition must have been amazing. You know, some people give great auditions but horrible performances. And vice versa. This must be the case with me and Jude, but even so, from a business perspective, I'm not going to sell any tickets.

So now, here I am in real life, impersonating an author.

So yeah, my dreams are definitely more interesting than my real life. But that's probably true for just about everyone. Who dreams of being themselves? When I'm just me in a dream, I'm usually terror-stricken and scrambling for my life, just beyond the threatening reach of some demon or villain. The scenarios are never sci-fi; they're a detour into the dark alleys of real life. Technically, that's a nightmare.

Back to Yogi's question: "What's the most interesting thing about you?" I can't imagine topping this story in real life or even in a dream. I met a friend of a friend one evening at dinner. I can't remember the details. I don't remember her name. However, I'll never forget that she had been lost at sea. Obviously, she survived. I could google the details of her story, but that's not critical to this story. You can do that on your own.

The point is: She had a defining moment that made her different than probably every other person she would ever meet. I'm not thinking I should get lost at sea, lost in the woods, or lost in space, but you can see the value in coloring outside the lines. I want to do things and make choices that will make my life one I want to remember.

I'm going to say yes to the things that may provide a good answer to the question, "What's the most interesting thing about you?"

But I will always say no to ayahuasca. I will never, ever opt for something that increases my chances of pooping in my pants. That's just not interesting.

"CHER CAN HOLD A PLANK POSE FOR FIVE MINUTES."

Did I hear that correctly?

When Cher was honored at the Billboard Music Awards in 2017, the seventy-one-year-old announced she could hold a plank pose for five minutes. The audience gave her lots of love for that.

I had a strong plank pose, but I couldn't compete with Cher.

A five-minute plank became a new goal.

I needed to work at it.

I had to work up to it.

There's no glory in a pose that incites panic in the body.

A pose works best when it's steady and calm.

When I finally matched Cher on the clock, I slowly lowered myself to the ground and drifted back into wide-legged child's pose. Breathe in to the count of eight. Hold. Breathe out to the count of eight. Repeat. On the next breath, I said to myself, *I'm never doing that again.*

And I never have.

Sometimes the shit you hear doesn't apply to you. I have a whole list of things I don't ever need to do to be a better person, even if they might be good for me:

- Go gluten-free
- Get ripped or shredded
- Live a vegan life

- Become proficient in another language, even though I wish I were
- Pretend to be a fan of *The Wire*
- Complete a marathon
- Reread anything I've read before even if I was too young to appreciate it
- Hike the Camino de Santiago in Spain

I started making lists in grammar school. I wasn't just making a list for Santa; I was in full life-management mode: movies I wanted to see, places I wanted to go, to-do lists, to-read lists, colleges to visit. At every age, packing for a trip required a list. I was never one to wing it. When it came to selecting a travel wardrobe, with my list, nothing was ever forgotten or missed. I was prepared with an outfit for any activity and all weather.

I developed a system of segmenting lists within lists: to do today, to do this week, to do short-term (a three-month outlook), and to do long-term (a twelve- to eighteen-month outlook). Those lists all lived within a bucket list—that go-for-it term that was popularized in 2006. I worked with a bucket list long before it was called a bucket list.

Having a list of goals can be motivating. It gets you organized. It helps get it all done. My type-A brain loves a list. I feel in control. Focused. Powerful. A man on a mission.

"Okay, do we all agree we'll go to Antarctica when you turn fifty-five?" That's me, chatting with some travel buddies, working the long-term plan. But time can run out when you least expect it.

I'm a recovering type-A, now happily rewired as a type-Y. A type-Y is guided (not driven) by a more chill, yoga-inspired energy. I now loathe the bucket list on my iPad. What was an organizing tool for future fun and adventure now reads like a torturous obligation. Only now can I appreciate that doing nothing *is*, in fact, doing something. Doing nothing is something I never got to do when work dominated my life. The bucket list just might be a young man's game. Young people have all the time in the world. With an iced matcha in hand, it's theirs to conquer. At my age, a bucket list becomes a lamentation on the things I may never get to do.

I used to study the curated lists of "Fifty Places to Visit This Year," "Best Books of the Last Ten Years," "Top Podcasts," "Must See This," and "Gotta Do That." I was well-acquainted with the "Most Anticipated New Restaurants" of the year. Now, I give them a tertiary review. When I realized the lists never get shorter, I surrendered to reality: I'll never have enough time to do everything that sounds interesting and go everywhere that promises excitement. And neither will you. I've freed myself from the tyranny of my bucket list. Recently, without any sense of ceremony, I've started taking things off my lists. Antarctica, I'll see you in the next life.

It's like they say at yoga: "Congratulate yourself for showing up to your mat." That's what I do every morning now; I show up for the day ahead. I don't try to max out every waking moment. I don't attempt to have "the most amazing weekend ever." Except for an occasional flare-up of anxiety, I've stopped biting my fingernails. Doesn't that say it all?

In the height of the summer traffic out here in the Hamptons, it's almost impossible to make a left-hand turn unless someone gives you the space. Now that I'm not racing against a clock, I frequently give people their moment to turn left.

Of course, every time I pause to give someone the right-of-way, someone else gives me the finger.

I'm so glad I'm not that person. As a type-Y, I no longer feel like I'm running out of time. Maybe I should take the time to do another five-minute plank. Not because I should. Just because I can.

"WE BEND SO WE DON'T BREAK."

Like palm trees, I thought to myself.

Palm trees go through hell, but they persevere. When the nightly news leads with hurricane footage from the Caribbean, the palm trees seem to say, "Fuck off," to the ninety-mile-an-hour winds. Their defiance is a marvel.

"We bend so we don't break."

It's a simple metaphor that celebrates a cunning flexibility.

When you give, you gain.

When a storm starts punching, palm trees bend. They survive. They live to see another day.

I take this imagery up into my first downward dog of the day.

This time the pose is less rigid, yet I feel stronger. More in control.

Message received: Don't fight the winds of change.

Give your life some sway even while you stand your ground.

If life is pushing you around, you can still weather the storm standing tall.

Is this yoga stuff starting to work for me?

"DO LESS. ALLOW MORE."

At its core, this is another way of saying, "Don't force a pose."

"Where you are today is where you need to be. Wherever you are is where the work needs to happen."

Yogi is talking to a small group this morning. The east end woke up to a driving rain, which always keeps people at home.

"The journey matters more than the destination…."

Blah, blah, blah…I got it.

"Do less. Allow more."

Sometimes, the same idea coming from a different voice lands with a crescendo of emotion of, *Aha! Oh, now I see….*

"Do less. Allow more."

In that moment, my yoga practice changed, and maybe my life shifted as well. I worked so *hard* to make difficult poses happen, but I was never rock-solid in the execution. My signature flourish was the face of constipation. All around me, yogis were at peace while I was at war with my body. I was fighting to reach beyond my reality.

Finally, I challenged myself to take this new approach.

"Allow more."

I did less. I allowed my body to find the pose.

Oddly, it required less effort.

This shift impacted work and life.

I spent my twenties, thirties, and forties carefully calculating and crafting strategic plans for my life, work, weekends, and vacations. I explored all options. I anticipated and game-planned against all outcomes. I was a magnet for anxiety. My effort always outweighed my results.

Subconsciously, I already knew this. It's exactly the same advice Regina George shared with Gretchen in *Mean Girls*: "Stop trying to make fetch happen."

For so much of my life, I was a Gretchen. I always wanted "fetch" to happen. The to-do list of prep and planning never got easier. Every idea was met with a chorus of "what-ifs." I exhausted myself in the pursuit of perfect.

I've always been envious of the "whatev" guys—guys whose lives just happen with very little preparation or disaster planning. Like cars, "whatev" guys come in various models: Birkenstock boys, fleece-vest preps, duffel-bag dudes, and the blue-eyed sparklers. They all wander out into the world expecting to have a nice day. Ad guys, tech guys, finance guys—they always meet you with a preoccupied stare. The "whatev" guys are like Labradors: walk them, charge their phones, feed them a burrito, and they're good to go. Even if their flight is delayed, they're chill. They rarely encounter consequences. I've always wanted to be that guy, but I'm not. At least, I wasn't.

Now, I do less and allow more. The choices I make have an easier fit. I find that what is effortless is, in fact, more enjoyable.

Do less. Allow more. The key to holding a pose is not *needing* to hold on to it. Like friendships, relationships, and jobs, yoga works best when you're relaxed in the pose.

For most of my adult life, I held onto friendships that consistently annoyed me. I congratulated myself for being a "good friend," working overtime to keep people in my life in spite of a persistent, knotted tangle in the relationship dynamic. At some point, I started to let those friendships fade away. Some people saw this as harsh. Cold. Uncaring. For me, it was a gesture of generosity. If these friendships weren't working for me, then they probably weren't working for the friend, either. Holding on to negatives gets in the way of gathering more positives. Trying to stay close to too many people gets in the way of being close with anybody at all.

It all became clearer and easier with the advent of Netflix. I was getting dressed, getting ready to meet friends for yet another dinner. I said to Randall, "If this dinner is nothing more than a review of what everyone has seen on Netflix, I'd rather stay home and curl up with a good series."

A simple criteria was born: *Do I really want to go to dinner and talk about ______?*

Fill in the blank:

"...Trump?"

"...real estate?"

"...the best time to be in St. Bart's?"

Or do I want to stay home and watch ______?

Fill in the blank:

"...*Ozark*?"

"...*Queen's Gambit*?"

"...*Homeland*?"

"...*Happy Valley*?"

"...*The Crown*?"

"...*Girls*?"

"...*Bad Sisters*?"

Use your own streaming list to fill in the blanks. This has become my new criteria when considering plans; the dinner has to be more interesting than an evening at home with *The Americans.* No judgment, but when I see friends now, it's because I love the conversation. I'm interested in their story. I no longer want more people; I want more of the people I adore.

"Do less. Enjoy everything more."

That's my new mantra, and I'm sticking with it.

"UN-RAZZLE-DAZZLE YOURSELVES."

That's the voice of a favorite yogi.

It's how she encourages students to release themselves from complicated poses. She's basically saying, "Keep it simple."

My face involuntarily registers a question mark.

"Michael, did I confuse you?"

"No—sneeze interrupted," I lied.

After class, I quietly asked, "I get the stuff you share at the top of class. I even keep a list of my faves. But what's wrong with the razzle-dazzle? I mean, I wish I could do some of the stuff...."

"Razzle-dazzle is there for the eye of the beholder. It has no real value. It's usually the former dancers. They'll always want to stand out from the chorus."

"Got it."

"Making the most of something doesn't always mean making more of it."

Not everything benefits from a flourish.

Razzle-dazzle can be fun. It can elevate the mundane. It can transform ordinary into extraordinary, even in small ways. Degree of difficulty is a key factor for athletes competing for Olympic gold. Points are given for building complication into a high dive or skating routine. But razzle-dazzle can also be distracting. Like too many pockets on a jacket.

The chronic pursuit of razzle-dazzle establishes an expectation that can be exhausting.

Look at Instagram and TikTok on a daily basis. You see how quickly razzle-dazzle loses its shine. In the visual streams of the carefully crafted and filtered content that populates social media platforms, when someone or something truly unique dances into your scroll, it's like finding gold twinkling in a sieve.

Somewhere in the world is a naturally cute and humpy construction worker. His first Insta post was a swivel-hipped little dance captured at a construction site. If you have a fetish for playful smiles and tool belts, this is the video you want to save. He was just having fun doing his thing without a nanosecond of self-consciousness. He obviously liked the tsunami of heart emojis that piled onto this video. Mine included. With each subsequent video that followed, you can see the failed effort to recapture the magic of his first impromptu post. His "dazzle" fades right before our very eyes. His calculation compromises his appeal. His adorable spirit is smothered by his growing need for adoration.

There are countless couples, coworkers, siblings, and friend groups whose dance videos quickly transform from unique blasts of fun, fun, fun into lifeless human wallpaper begging to be seen. The endless stream of models, fashionistas, and hot bodies has become an extended pageant with no winner. The me-me-me monologists who go viral in a moment eventually run out of things worth saying. That's doesn't stop them from broadcasting uninspired opinions. They are a twenty-first century Willy Loman, knocking on your digital door, selling themselves by the click. Attention must be monetized.

Instagram is an endless parade of self-consciousness, except for the dog videos. They're always and truly a-dog-able. Dogs don't think about their image. They are not in the business of their personal brand. Dogs on social are pure joy, unencumbered by calculation. They can't manufacture a moment for the camera. They never try to razzle-dazzle us. Dogs don't count likes and shares. They don't apply filters to change their eye color. You don't have to reassure them that they're hot. If you feed a dog, it's happy. That construction worker had the same spirit as an Instagram puppy, until he got into the business of being liked.

Sarah Cooper figured it out. Her first couple of tweets lip-syncing to the insanity and inanity of Donald Trump came to us from comedy heaven. Conceptually unique. Brilliant execution. Genius timing. For many, she justified the existence of Twitter. Sarah instinctively knew when to stop. She wasn't going to beg for more attention than the joke deserved. Sarah knew exactly when to un-razzle-dazzle herself.

It goes back to the cliché: Less is more. At the root of every cliché is an obvious truth: Happy, sexy, and cool don't require a look that's big, grand, and dramatic. There is power in simplicity. It's why a little black dress has always been in style. Simplicity is how Apple and Everlane don't just have customers, they have rabid and loyal enthusiasts.

There is beauty and brilliance in just being.

If you've been running a fast race, it takes a while to cool down. We all have moments when the solutions feel as complicated as the challenges. We want to charge forward and slay the dragon. The better solution might be to cool down and tackle the complications with an easy, steady pace.

So I go to yoga, knowing that it works best to just be there for myself, no razzle-dazzle required.

The more I did yoga, the more I became swaddled in a physical calm. My body wasn't worried about itself. The poses had more ease and less effort. As I built a greater command of my physical state, I developed a stronger hold on a calmer state of mind.

Months later, heading into class, yogi and I entered at the same time.

"I love this!" she said, gesturing a circle around my upper body.

"My beanie?"

"No. Your vibe is different. You enter the room differently."

"Hmm. How so?"

"I see calm."

"Is that your sixth sense?" The movie pun fell flat.

"Being at ease in your world requires physical and emotional calm. One feeds the other. Yoga's working for you, my friend."

"Aha—there it is!" That's me, finally, really getting it.

Razzle-dazzle is not in the effort, it's in the result. Calm is more impressive—more powerful—than any degree of razzle-dazzle.

Calm is a great way to stand out from the chorus.

In the midst of buzzy beings, calm can make you a singular sensation.

"DON'T OVERACHIEVE."

Again—this yoga stuff is sometimes counterintuitive.

Me talking to me again.

Don't overachieve. Anybody ever say that to you? A teacher? A coach? A parent?

Nope. Never. Definitely not my dad.

Dad was a true Catholic, and by that I mean everything was transactional. If you sin, ten Hail Marys grants you absolution. If you sin big time, you burn in hell. Do good, and you get into heaven. Dad's path to heaven was transactional.

1. Every Sunday, Bill Norton dropped a wad of cash into the collection plate at nine o'clock mass.
2. Dad kept the parish rectory and convent stocked with liquor; it's the least he could do since he owned three liquor stores. He'd personally drop a few cases every month so parishioners would never see a Norton's Cork'n Bottle van making a blessed delivery.
3. He also hand-delivered turkeys, shrimp, and a case of Mateus wine on the eves of Thanksgiving and Christmas. For the Saint Philip and Saint James nuns and priests, Dad was heaven-sent. I'll tell you, good deeds do not a good Catholic make. If there is a god, my dad's in hell, mistakingly assigned to the nonsmoking section.

When I was seventeen, heaven was a bong. I smoked a lot of pot. I got stupid, as potheads do.

One day, as I was rolling into fifth period after lunch, Sister Virginia Lolloway caught my glassy-eyed daze. Nuns know everything.

"Mr. Norton—twelve times twelve?"

"Whaaaat?"

"Mr. Norton, is 'whaaaat' your only answer to a question?"

That nun actually imitated my stoner slur. She knew. Nuns weren't stupid. When you're stoned, the obvious always seems hilarious. Of course, I answered, "Whaaaat?"

That sent my stoner buddies into fits of laughter and imitation.

When a nun loses control of her classroom, they don't fight the moment. They start playing the long game, plotting the most effective revenge.

I assume when my dad handed over a case of Chablis at the convent's back door that Mateus-loving nun mentioned in passing that I wasn't "focused."

I assume it went something like this:

"He's a smart boy, but lately you'd think he had"—in a calculated whisper—"shit for brains."

Yes, nuns understand the impact of colorful language.

One night, around 11:00 p.m., I was in bed reading, probably *Helter Skelter*. I devoured anything that played out in the fringes of a lurid lifestyle: *The Onion Field*, *The Other Side of Midnight*, *In Cold Blood.* I lived for the "Justice Story" in the *New York Daily News*. This was a center spread in the Sunday paper that chronicled the "true crime tales of murder, mystery and mayhem." In my tween years, I wanted to be kidnapped and become the subject of an intense manhunt. Of course, I assumed I'd just be watching TV until the ransom was paid. I'd be kept in the basement of an old farmhouse tucked away in the blistering cold of one of the Dakotas. Upon rescue, I'd emerge, ready for my very own "Justice Story."

If the internet had existed in the late 1960s, I would have been an easy target for any troll looking for young, impressionable prey. Reading *On the Road* fueled my fantasy of taking off, running away, hitting the road. I wasn't stupid, but if I had access to a chat room, I definitely could have been coaxed into meeting a stranger at the Arby's on Route 22, excited to take off for a super cool summer in California. I desperately wanted to be some sort of hippie. But clean. A clean hippie. Like a hippie you'd see in a television show. Instead, I probably would have been hog-tied in the trunk and driven to Indianapolis. I would have spent the next three years in a drugged daze working hard for the money as a hustler at the Greyhound bus depot. I don't think the "Justice Story" editors would have gone with a story about strung out teen trade. *Taxi Driver* didn't arrive in theaters until 1976.

Back to Dad. He walked by my bedroom. We hadn't crossed paths in maybe a week. That was normal and okay. But at that moment he stuck his head in the door.

"Deliver the A's. Nobody gets anywhere by striving for less."

No, my dad wasn't a philosopher. And that didn't sound like my dad. But there was more.

"You'll want to get up earlier tomorrow. You'll be walking to school. Leave your car keys on the dining table."

Dad giveth, and Dad taketh away.

My dad gave his three boys cars. Not his daughters. Just his boys. It wasn't generosity. It was control. Very transactional, like a good Catholic.

I also realized my dad never thought about why I wasn't focused. It never occurred to him that his son was a stoner. He just wanted the A's.

Walking to school is a great time to get stoned. Or think.

Reaching for the middle seems void of inspiration, right?

Eventually, I got the wisdom in this.

A buzz was fun, but the car was freedom.

Smoke less, drive more.

Sounds like: *Do less. Allow more.*

If you push a yoga pose too hard, you can push your body into a space it's not prepared to go.

Without the proper stretch, reach, and support, you're setting yourself up for a long-term relationship with a chiropractor, trigger-point injections, and Voltaren. In your desire to do "more," you may overreach.

Don't overachieve.

A solid base and steady build are essential prep for every advance.

It's like building too much into a travel itinerary: Trying to see too much always leads to cranky lunches and tired-face pictures. Joy lives in the unstructured time. That's where spontaneous whims wait for us.

If you try so hard to succeed at everything, you might miss your life. Or at least, some of the good parts.

Overachievers are never happy. They have lots of associates, but they rarely have true friends.

If you've seen *Election*, you know this to be true.

I'm not suggesting we all start underachieving.

I'm not making a big push for mediocrity.

Slacker energy has never been sexy.

It's just a simple formula: Don't outrun the pace of life.

The real win is often something that can't be quantified.

"Be careful of the detour presented by ambition," said somebody somewhere. It's in my phone notes, but the source is unknown. It may be me.

"KNOW LESS."

Self to self: *Is this* Yoga for Dummies*? She did say, "Know less," didn't she?*

"I'm not the first to say it. Learning is a lifelong process."

I heard it again, a calm and reassuring, "Know less."

I went to Catholic school—I've always followed direction, seriously intent on avoiding the harrowing glare and slap-happy hand of a cross-eyed nun. Nuns often reacted with a hot fury better suited to a career in Roller Derby.

"Know less."

Over the next few classes, she kept saying it, like a mantra.

I struck an active listening pose.

In yoga, experience tells our body what to do and *not* do in a pose. Rigid boundaries can make it almost impossible for your body to do anything new. To go where it hasn't been. To stretch. To grow. To learn something new about itself. Your body has things to tell you as it reaches for its limits.

For most yogis, handstands and headstands aren't a big deal. For me, they are the impossible dream. Also, I have Barrett's syndrome (industrial strength acid reflux), so the good doctor has cautioned that an inversion isn't such a smart move for me. One unremarkable day, this happened: Without expectation or anticipation, without thinking about it so intently, without working so hard at it, I threw myself up into a handstand. It's wasn't perfect. It wasn't pretty. But for a brief moment, I was there. It's a pose I haven't been able to repeat. It happened because I wasn't thinking. I wasn't reminding myself of my limitations. I forgot my fear. I wasn't stuck in my I-can't-do-this-pose mindset. In that unconscious attempt at a handstand, my body had more power over my mind.

The downside of a handstand is that after a certain age, if you're upside down, the skin on your legs develops a disgusting crepe. However, that fleeting and surprising inversion illustrates that you don't have to make everything happen—sometimes you can just let it happen. My head wasn't the boss of me. In the moment, I knew less. Knowing less that day allowed me to learn more.

It can be equally beneficial to "know less" in our social, emotional, and professional lives. Yes—experience should prepare us and guide us, but it shouldn't limit us.

We've all been taught to never judge a book by its cover. Knowing or assuming less opens you up to learning more. Entering that room with "now what?" curiosity is a more optimistic space, ripe with the possibility of meeting something unexpected.

For me, that handstand signals that there are surprises still to come.

Who knows? Maybe somebody will enjoy this book. I could let the probability of rejection bring an end to this right now. How much time have I given to this big unknown?

Maybe I need to know less about how this will all end? Maybe I'll be surprised.

"KEEP WHAT YOU LOVE."

These words from a very unassuming yogi upstate hit an immediate bull's-eye.

I was so lost in this thought I got stuck in cat/cow while everyone else moved on to sun salutations.

I can't stop my mind from racing....

I spend ridiculous amounts of energy trying to hold on to things that are already gone. Clothes that don't fit. An old dopp kit stuffed with skin-care samples that never get used. Long-standing friendships that no longer click.

I hoard memories that retain their sting. I try and fail to purge the festering emotions stuffed into the recesses of my mind.

So, I try this.

I set up a yard sale in my head of all the people who fall into the "friends" category. Then I identify the "keepers"—the ones I love. The friends who make me like myself.

Then I tag the people who are "easy mixers." Uncomplicated and always fun. They're definitely worth more time.

A few friends need to be repurposed. Their friendship is rooted in who we were, not who we are today. If friendships are stuck in the glow of your "hilarious" past, it might be time to make the move from "then" to "now." Hopefully, who you are now is more interesting than the person who lives on Memory Lane. It's okay to stay in touch with the past, but an occasional email might work better than faking your way through a withering connection.

"Keep what you love."

It's easy to identify the friends who aren't real friends. They require management. Honesty isn't easy. Conversations have sand traps. The time you spend is tinged with regret.

Whether physical objects or personal relationships, if it isn't "value-added," then there's no reason to keep it in your life. And even if the friend you've tagged for Goodwill doesn't know that, it's probably true for them too.

Suddenly, class is winding down. I love when a class ends, not because it's over but because of how stretched and strong I feel. And yoga lightens my heart. I realize, I'm okay that running is in my past. Sure, on a sunny, seventy-degree day, when I see a runner in full stride, I'm shot through with envy. I can feel his exhilaration. But it's fleeting. That was then, this is now. And right now, I'm loving that I added yoga to my life. For me, yoga is a keeper.

"SMART PEOPLE KEEP IT SIMPLE."

My favorite yoga teachers keep it simple.

Adjustments are clear.

They don't talk to me about a *drishti*; they just tell me what to move where.

"Pull your left hip back. You want a straight line across your hips."

"Ahh—much more stable. Thank you."

It's actionable and effective.

Here's a simple adjustment I gave myself: If I fuck up, I just say so. Sometimes, instead of a simple, "I fucked up," people fall into an overcomplicated overanalysis of the why. That's just a way of saying, "I fucked up but it wasn't really my fault so I wasn't really wrong and you should understand."

Smart people just say, "I fucked up. Sorry."

It's that simple. Or should be.

There's this guy I sort of admire and despise him in equal measure. He's fired people, ended relationships and berated waiters with unnecessary and harsh severity. Not nice. Before you can even question his behavior, he intercepts the criticism by openly declaring, "I'm a dick." He distills it down to the truth of the matter, leaving nothing to analyze, explain, discuss or argue about. For him, there's no story to tell. It is that simple: he is a dick. I don't admire his character, but his clarity is unexpected and disarming. Is that a smart way to live? Is he happy? Only he can answer that question but while everyone scrambles to pick up the pieces, while they debate the rot of his heart and soul, he's already moved on, ego intact. His life is all forward motion. I don't want to be known as a dick, but I'd like to engineer more efficiency into my emotional contractions.

Smart people don't get caught up in the complications. They journey forward, following the trail of facts and insights. Decisions almost write themselves.

Problems persist because people get stuck in their stories. They get trapped in the "he said/she said/they said" scenarios. They get lost in the what, when, and why. What's in between is distraction, complicating the ability to make decisions. Ultimately, truth hides in the emotion of a situation. It's not the facts that matter, it's the feelings. Are you happy or not happy?

Smart people don't get trapped by the past, fooled by the future, or lost in the present. Smart people don't trip over "if only" or "what if."

When my contract at Disney wasn't renewed, I was lost in a storm of anger, confusion, fear, and sadness. I replayed the story of the evil-queen executive over and over in my head, but that never changed the outcome.

When my movie went into turnaround at Warner Bros., it felt like the end of a Looney Tunes cartoon with Porky Pig telling me, "That's all Folks!" I didn't want my Hollywood story to end there. But it did.

When client relationships and ad agency positions ended, they rarely ended on a happy note. No matter how many times I reviewed the stories, I never felt better.

My last corporate gig was Global Creative Director on Maybelline NY. I knew this story wouldn't last even before I started. Beware of the people who tell you how nice they are. Typically, they are the human equivalent of poison ivy. But this time, my story was simple. I needed to keep the job until the mortgage on my house was approved. The day we closed on our home was my last day trying to convince women that a longwear lipstick was their bridge to a happy life. I left that job knowing I got exactly what I wanted. I wasn't stuck in a story that held no promise of joy or satisfaction. I wasn't wondering what happened, what went wrong, or what might have been. For the first time, my happy heart trumped my hungry ego. It was over and out.

My story didn't belong to Disney, Hollywood, or Maybelline.

If I had hung on to my old story, if I had fought for another position as a creative director, I'd be in a totally different story. I may not have found yoga again. I doubt I'd be writing this book. I'd be compromised by the needs of ego and image. I suspect I wouldn't like who I would have become.

As the yogi suggested, by keepin' it simple, the adjustments in life are clear.

"APPRECIATION OF WHAT YOU HAVE IS THE BEST PROFIT IN LIFE."

S*uze Orman?* I wondered.

Could be Tony Robbins? I countered.

I think, *Deepak Chopra?*, even though I doubted it.

Was this a Peanuts *cartoon?*, hit like a eureka moment.

Peanuts! It does sound kind of twee, I had to admit.

There's my cynicism elbowing its way back into yoga class.

I googled it on my phone in the parking lot. Nothing.

So yeah, it made sense, and it was a nice thought, and even if people did appreciate what they have, they've been programmed to want more. Even your average yogi has an extensive wardrobe of leggings, crop tops, crochet shrugs, and flowery tattoos.

But something's happening. There's a growing movement around convincing people to want less.

When perusing knitwear (a.k.a. sweaters) on Mr. Porter, I'm always stoked when I add one to my cart. But recently, I'm equally happy when there's nothing I have to have. Is it starting? Am I evolving? Am I learning to appreciate what I have and not crave what I don't have?

Admittedly, and contrary to my much-younger self, I am perfectly happy being home on a Friday night. Or any night for that matter. My FOMO has transformed into FOGO—fear of going out.

A few years ago, on the first day of my first staycation, I woke up with a big inhale. No packing. No airport. No worrying about my dog. For most of my adult life, I had felt shamefully, apologetically incomplete because I hadn't been to Bhutan. Hadn't Bhutan become just a commercialized version of its former self? I didn't know, and I was not flying a day and a half to find out.

I channeled my inner Buddhist monk: "Learning to want less is the bridge to more time in peaceful bliss."

Was yoga making me philosophical?

My social animal roared back, *Enough with the yoga. You are in grave danger of waking up with a gray ponytail and a hemp wardrobe!*

My inner yogi fought back with a dose of intentional calm. *No. When you want less, you spend more time in the moment. That's when you feel most alive.*

The conversation with myself heated up.

So, we're good? It's okay to skip Bhutan. It's okay to do nothing?

Remember, doing nothing is doing something. By doing nothing, you'll have time to appreciate all that you have.

Do not *talk like this at a dinner party. Ever. This platitudinal shit stays between us!*

Well, when people read the book, they might ask about it.

They'll want to know about Steve Bannon. Talk about him. Tell Hollywood stories. Arnell stories. Nun stories. Promise you won't start talking like a guru from another planet.

I am clearly not my own best friend.

Just like there's a business in helping people get rid of their shit, there's probably money to be made coaching people how to do nothing.

As I write this, I'm sitting on a plane. We left JFK four hours and fifteen minutes ago enroute to PSP—Palm Springs International Airport. The woman next to me has been juggling her phone, computer, raisin bagel, and multiple bags of potato chips nonstop. Her hands have not stopped moving the entire flight. She has frantically searched furniture, chandeliers, drop earrings, silk tank tops, wine, shearling vests, Moroccan recipes, pantone colors, mascaras, ballet flats, pickle ball skirts, restaurants, nail art, Eras tour tickets on StubHub, and something about

Seussical the Musical. She's been writing (actually pounding out) about eleven emails per hour and has *tap-tap-tapped* through her Insta and Facebook feeds. She's rabidly hearted, DM'd, saved, shared, commented, and commented on comments. Her feet and her seat are surrounded by a flood of tote bags full of stuff—it's like Mother Courage scored a mileage upgrade.

My eyes hurt from trying really hard to get lost in my book.

From what my left eye was able to glean, her sole purpose with this escape to Palm Desert is to float in her parent's pool so she's tan for her sister's wedding.

This woman could be the beta test for my idea of the nothing coach. Beyond meditation. Beyond a spa day. Like so many people, her mind will never quiet itself. She'll never smell the roses or hear the lullaby of waves rolling onto shore. She'll never even hear her own thoughts. Death will be her only ticket to peace of mind. When she passes, her fingers will twitch well beyond her last breath.

Looking across the aisle at this wild-eyed, rabid keyboarding woman, I saw me from the not-too-distant past, always looking, wanting, searching, hoping for something more. There was a constant pursuit of cool. To be in the know. To be there first. To have some feeling of having it all.

Suddenly, I have a more profound appreciation for what yogi said.

"The appreciation for what you have..."

Ten years ago, if this plane was going down, I'd be angry at everything I'd be about to lose. The things I'd never get to do. The years I'd never enjoy. But now, I think about my husband, my dog, our home, our friends. I appreciate how lucky I've been. Maybe I didn't get everything I wanted, but besides a few EGOT winners, who does?

On the other hand, if my fellow traveler across the aisle senses that our final destination today is that light at the end of the tunnel, she'll probably google, "Top ten things to do in the afterlife."

"WE'RE GOING TO MAKE LOVE TO OUR JOINTS. DO YOU LOVE YOUR BIG TOE ENOUGH?"

I'm in the wrong class.

Palm Springs can be like that.

"LET'S GET OUR BODY READY FOR THE RAIN."

It's the desert. Even a sprinkle is a big deal.

Wrong class again.

"BE CAREFUL NOT TO SPEND TOO MUCH TIME IN THE PAST. IT WAS NEVER WHAT YOU REMEMBER."

I have many friends who, after kids and careers, move back to New York looking for their past. They imagine pickup games in the park and stumbling into conversations with Debbie Harry or Julian Schnabel at BAM. They want to recapture who they were when they were twenty-seven. That was thirty-five years ago. That you doesn't exist anymore. And that New York—their New York—doesn't exist anymore either. In fact, they complain about it all the time. They see the ghosts of the stores, bars, and bodegas that no longer exist. They remember the underground fringes that made them cool. What was home to the Tunnel and your evening of debauchery is now part of a gentrified neighborhood where Martha Stewart is headquartered and art galleries peddle million-dollar paintings.

When I walk to the river on an April weekend, I pass spaces that were the smoke-filled restaurants of my sonic youth. Today, they are juice bars and yoga studios. Rather than Leigh Bowery–inspired club kids fighting the burn of sunlight, the must-have accessory on a Saturday morning is a yoga mat.

Big cities. Small towns. They evolve. They don't stand still just so you can live in the past. Nothing ages you more in the eyes of the beholder than a those-were-the-days conversation.

To appreciate the past, you had to be there.

And as I've learned in yoga, to appreciate the present, you have to be here.

“UNCLOUD.”

On that note, class begins.

No one had ever heard yogi say this.

He lets the uncertainty linger.

There is a collective shift to curiosity.

We all feel better knowing that we’re in the dark together.

Yogi smiles and enlightens us.

“Dogs frequently do resets. You’ve seen it. They root themselves on the floor and do a fast shakeout of their whole body.”

He demonstrates. He loves his stage.

“‘Uncloud’ is a human reset. Plant your feet, breathe in, and just throw your head and shoulders around in all directions. You’ll feel like you just woke up and the gunk of life will seem to be gone.”

We follow, willingly. The room sounds like a grammar school playground but with deeper voices.

Yogi lives for the childlike moments he unleashes.

This morning, everything was wrong. There was carnage in the backyard; a hawk got his claws into a rabbit. The electrician texted, “Can’t make today. Maybe next week.” Two driveway lights have been out for six months. Optimum was still billing me for a cable box I returned eight weeks ago. And I had forgotten to pick up yogurt, so breakfast sucked.

I unclouded with a fury.

I found the rainbow. Since I didn't have breakfast, I get to have a *pain au chocolate* on the way home after class.

Works for me.

Uncloud.

It may not solve all of life's problem, but it gets rid of stupid stuff.

Dogs know shit.

"APPRECIATE WHAT YOU GET, NOT WHAT YOU DON'T GET."

Martha's Vineyard. The studio has a definitive patchouli vibe. I still can't believe Carly Simon didn't join the class. Lots of earrings that looked like dreamcatchers.

Upon entering, most people seem to bathe in essential oils.

A young woman with glassy eyes stares down the room; the locals know it's time to begin. She must have worked in fashion.

"Appreciate what you get, not what you don't get."

I know she was encouraging us to appreciate what is physically available to us and not dwell on the limits of our practice. This was a clear signal that there were some superadvanced yogis in the room and no one should be intimidated. I suspected that at some point, the woman in leaf green ombre leggings was going to freelance into a scorpion handstand. It's fine, I'm not here to compete. I'm here for me. *Am I in proximity to peace of mind?*

Sometimes, what I hear in yoga transports me directly into my personal issues.

I don't know a single person in advertising who hasn't, at some point, questioned their role in promoting unchecked consumerism. The entire industry is designed to create desire. I'm certain there were endless meetings, reams of research, eager creative teams, and ample budgets all working to convince their target consumer that they needed, wanted, and were going to love:

- Bubble Gum vodka
- Cheetos lip balm
- Harley-Davidson perfume
- Crystal Pepsi—the clear cola
- Lifesaver soda

Unless you escape to a hermetically sealed existence, you will never have everything you want as long as marketers can grab your eyeballs.

Desire can be a great motivator, inspiring us to reach beyond current limitations. But a constant craving can eat you alive. When we focus on what we don't have, we forget to enjoy what we do have.

Not surprisingly, there were earrings and essential oils for sale after class.

As I exit, Yogi offers a spritz of some magical mix of essential oils.

I'm all in.

I admit, a spritz of lavender, mandarin, rosewood, and palmarosa can be all I need to shift my mood.

"WE'LL BEGIN IN FIVE."

I'm always early for class. I claim my spot next to a window. I am not a center-of-the-room guy. I sit on a block and scroll through notes on my phone. There's always something I forgot to do. I come across these three aphorisms straight out of the mouths of yogis.

When I get home, I transfer them to post-its. The post-its are then transferred to a moleskin notebook that is the keeper of ideas and inspiration I want to remember forever but never look at again.

"EFFORTLESS EFFORT."

I like this. Whether tackling a yoga pose or just living life, only do the work that's necessary to the task. Eliminating struggle doesn't compromise the achievement.

"DON'T LET EMOTION GET IN THE WAY OF WISDOM."

I do this all the time. No. I did *this all the time. Not so much now. Must be the yoga.*

"YOU CAN'T STOP AGING, BUT YOU DON'T HAVE TO GET OLDER."

Or is it, "You're going to get older, but you don't have to age." Either way, it's the same advice. There comes a time to *not* act your age. And yoga is a great way to keep your body younger than its age.

"WHAT YOU RESIST WILL PERSIST!"

The yogi just stepped on my Achilles heel.

#procrastination! would be the hashtag under my silent scream.

"In your practice, when you're on the mat, the space that's challenging is where the good work lives."

The woman in front of me was head-nodding like an overcaffeinated acolyte, letting everyone know that *she* got it. If you could've read my mind, you'd have heard, *Oh, her again. She drives me—stop—attitude check. (Silent "om.")*

"Avoidance is never a solution. There are very few things in life that go away on their own."

Well, that I agree with.... Although I had a nun that always said, "If you worry about it, it won't happen." I'm not sure where she found that. Gotta be the New Testament.

Procrastination is normal; after all, no one likes cleaning up a mess.

There's always tomorrow. Or next week. Or never.

But life's irritants persist. Even the tiniest bit of "suckiness" is something we hope and pray will, magically, resolve itself.

- Disturbing rashes;
- Unmanageable closets;
- Overstuffed cabinets; and
- If you're still analog, that pile of newspapers you'll never read.

They persist—these low-grade irritants. Ignoring them is impossible.

And then there are the:

- Uncomfortable conversations
- Emotional stews
- Perceived slights

They're there, haunting you. Taunting you.

They swim around in your head and steal your focus. They can make you miss your exit on the LIE or your stop on the downtown six-train.

Inevitably, there are personal and professional relationships that need a tune-up. Whatever remains unsaid is always the elephant in the room, holding you hostage until you speak your mind. Some relationships may have reached their expiration date, but they still deserve a conversation. A respectful end. An understanding.

We get stuck in an internal dialogue trying to understand what's not working with friends, bosses, coworkers, and siblings. It's easy to overanalyze the feelings and disappointments, but, really, it's quite simple: We change, they change, and the world changes.

You may have a friend you met when you lived in LA, but if you met them today, you wouldn't become friends.

You may have a boss who was the mentor you needed when you took your first "real" job. Now, that "greatest boss ever" can't see that you're ready to lead. In fact, without knowing it, they may resent that you no longer require their tutelage.

Siblings grow up together, but they can also grow apart. Blood is not always thicker than a fight over a will.

The promise of "forever and ever" keeps many couples together, but it can't always keep them close. Feeling lonely in a relationship is a sadness so deep you can drown in the silence.

When the joy of a relationship starts to evaporate, the air gets increasingly uncomfortable. Conversations are pockmarked by annoyances. Sometimes, small differences become infuriating divides. When key relationships lose their luster, too often, we avoid the inevitable conclusion. The "unspoken" festers, forcing us to swim through the seas of confusion, sadness, anger, and loss. Our resistance to a direct and honest conversation often prompts an unfortunate and irreparable end.

Why don't some of my friends like me anymore?

I've been haunted by this question now and then.

And why, suddenly, don't I like some of my friends?

This bothered me a great deal until I dove into it. Deeply.

Friends are like sweaters: A few I'll wear till the day I die, or the sweater is ravaged by a pack of lucky moths. Others only get trotted out once or twice a season. And then there's a few each year that, for some reason, don't look like me now. Those sweaters go to Housing Works, where they will find new friends. Extrapolating this metaphor into other areas of my life, I've become more accepting of the ebb and flow of friendships.

Admittedly, I know I irritate some people. But I think it could be for the same reasons that other people might be drawn to me. Just like the clothes in my closet, friends need to fit to feel good. I no longer lose sleep over what isn't; I prefer to dream about what's to come. Standing still has never put me in the path of new friends. Another Hallmark moment, but sometimes, it is what it is.

"What you resist will persist!"

Even the tiniest fracture in a relationship must be attended to. It will not go away on its own.

There's a good amount of research that explores the dynamics of friendship.

In her *New York Times* article, "The Pandemic Shrank Our Social Circles. Let's Keep It That Way," Kate Murphy wrote, "Several studies show we replace *as much as half* of our social network every five to seven years. Little wonder when research also shows only half of our friendships are *mutual.* That is, only half of those who we think are our friends feel the same way about us. It just normally takes us a while to figure that out."

We've all had situational friends—people from school, work, or the neighborhood—with whom the connection evaporates when daily routines no longer intersect. Happily, they are deposited in the bank of fond memories.

In his research on our personal relationships, Robin Dunbar, the British anthropologist, found that the average adult sheds a friendship every 2.3 years. I'm living proof of that theory. I've shed some very good friends on a pretty regular basis. When I turned fifty, I started the shift from quantity to quality.

Like water evaporating on a summer sidewalk, many friendships end without much notice. Sadly, there are a few friendships that end badly. Perhaps they need to end badly. I have a collection of people formerly known as a "best friend" with whom there is no communication. There's really no desire to even attempt a renewal. Perhaps, when strong connections break, even gorilla glue can't put it back together. With these friends, I admit, I avoided listening to my instincts. I would meet those friends, not with genuine enthusiasm, but rather, with the burden of obligation.

We've been friends for thirty years! I'd say to myself as a way to inflate any sense of attachment.

We just need a good catch-up! allowed me to temporarily feign an effortless and seamless connection.

My god, we traveled to China together, was my way of resisting that it was time to let go.

I never, ever, *ever* want my world to change. I want to know that everything in life that's good and joyous will stay that way forever. I'm a friends-are-everything kind of guy, so how can it ever be okay to lose one? But I've seen that losing a friend is the prerequisite for finding an even better friend that's a better fit for right now.

In yoga, your relationship with a pose requires mutual respect. You can't cheat it. The full expression of the pose is where you'll find the most benefit. If you're not in it 100 percent, the pose will be your enemy.

I hate Warrior 2. It's not a hard pose at all, but I loathe standing there with my arms extended at shoulder height. Cheating the pose with lazy extremities doesn't make it easier. Nothing will ever make me love that pose, but I know that when I commit 100 percent to the fullness of the pose, I hate it less. In yoga, without that 100 percent commitment to a pose, the result will be slouchy and schlumpy. You'll be the distracting, wobbly one—an irritation to the steadfast warriors all around you.

Giving less than 100 percent to your personal and professional relationships will also result in wobbly outcomes. Rather than energizing conversations, every interaction will feel lumpy and dumpy.

In yoga, there is no finish line. No matter what you accomplish, there's always the next level, which may be as simple as holding that pose for another five seconds.

Here's my goal:

Yogi says, "Cartwheel your hands and open up into Warrior 2."

I don't say, *I hate this shit,* inside my head.

I've had friendships that suddenly felt like Warrior 2 to me. I wasn't giving it 100 percent.

Holding onto relationships is a survival instinct. It's the instinct to build a protective community. To create a sense of belonging.

Relationships can hold us in a place where we no longer belong.

Less resistance. More acceptance.

Life evolves, if you let it.

"IT'S OKAY TO BE AFRAID, BUT YOU DON'T HAVE TO REACT TO IT."

Afraid?

That's an odd start to a yoga class. Then it hits me.

Teach is talking to me.

It's my fear of doing inversions (handstands and headstands). We've determined that I'm strong enough to go upside down, but I'm defeated by my fear. She's right; rather than focusing on the mechanics of the pose, I am reacting to the image of spending my summer in a neck brace.

With a surge of gusto, yogi declares, "Fear is not a problem. Fear is a natural response to potential threats."

I'm not the only person stymied by today's inspirational tidbit. It requires elaboration.

Everyone has their high-alert moments:

– A deer darts in front of your car.
– An adrenalin-fueled seventeen-year-old in his father's Datsun weaves a crazy path through rush hour traffic.
– A sore in your mouth prompts sleepless prayers that it's not related to the sex you had last week.

In situations such as these, fear is natural, but it's your reaction that can be deadly.

In a tense situation, fear can cloud your judgement and compromise your ability to determine the optimal response. By maintaining control of your reaction (and your car), you assert power over your fear and avoid making a bad move.

Fear is human. It's healthy—it saves us from bear attacks, scam artists, and stupid decisions.

Our unique collection of fears and insecurities serves as our GPS for navigating life. I always push forward with a force field of confidence and determination. But fears are like viruses; as you conquer them, they evolve into new variants.

In my twenties and thirties, I had slowly shed the insecurities of youth that linger until we're solid with who we are. It took me a while to see who I was instead of what I wasn't. But with each accomplishment in life, I would then lose sleep worrying about losing what I had gained.

My forties were consumed with financial fears. I was broke once and never wanted to be that powerless again. When I say broke, I mean in debt, with nothing coming in. As my career (finally) advanced, I lived in fear of taking two steps backward. Fear propelled me forward with a focused velocity (finally). Then, later in my fifties, I'd wake up every morning and stare down new insecurities. As age began its slow creep across my face and body, I sensed hairline fractures in my psyche. This fear was new. Trickier. This wasn't about age spots or fine lines; Fraxel and Botox could quiet those concerns. This was a fear rooted in the unknown. I was idling in neutral, not knowing where I wanted to go in life. My self-image was at least ten years younger than my reality. I wasn't in control of what happened next. If you lose a job, you know that finding the next one is your immediate focus. It's unsettling when you sense that all of your experience may not be what people are looking for now. If your relationship ends, you force yourself back in the game, even though you're shocked how much the mating dance has changed. If you're gay, now you need a dick-pic. If you're straight, admit it, you probably have a dick-pic too. But when your vitality starts to wane, you feel like you're inhabiting a ghost. When your sense of purpose starts to shrink, if you're anything like me, you'll feel caught in a limbo between life and death. Nobody ever blew out sixty candles on a birthday cake and crowed, "Yay! Finally, no one gives a shit what I think! Here's to irrelevance!"

Even worse, there comes the first time you say, "Grab the six-thirty reservation. The eight fifteen feels too late to sit down to dinner."

WTF?! You grab for an imaginary handrail. *Dinner at 6:30 p.m?! That's very close to the edge of tragic.*

True if you live in New York, but not if you live in the rest of America.

Naturally, as a marketer, I see my challenge clearly. I want peace. I want calm. I want my Cialis outdoor bathtub moments. "Serenity Now" becomes the mission.

I won't become a middle-aged poodle, easily identified by too many "dermatological" processes or age-inappropriate fashion.

I don't want nights where "just one cocktail" sloshes into four because, "Why not…? Nothing critical on the docket tomorrow."

Step one: Listen up at yoga. You don't know what you don't know.

Step two: Get real. Don't fight an unwinnable war.

Step three: Make friends with my fears; otherwise, fear is driving the bus.

"ORGANIZE YOUR FACE."

Not surprisingly, this Los Angeles yogi offers up a little cosmetic philosophy. Judging by the amount of filler in the room, she knows her audience. But there's something to her outside-in advice.

If the eyes are the window into your soul, then sure, your face telegraphs exactly what you're thinking and feeling at any given moment.

Similar to how you can flip the orientation on your phone's camera, you can use your face to be the boss of what you're feeling.

Tense?

Scared?

Slightly sad?

Use your face to redirect what you're feeling inside. Project the opposite, and you'll start to be it.

Conversely, sometimes your face isn't in sync with what you are feeling. On many occasions, I've been asked "What's wrong?" even though there isn't a problem. Nothing's wrong. I'm just deep in thought. Apparently, my "concentration face" looks like mental constipation.

"Organize your face" became my mantra for that class.

When I sensed a self-inflicted scrunchy face during a shaky Warrior 3, I forced a smile. My new face instantly made me feel brighter and lighter.

With a calm face, I was more in control of my pose.

I'd been tightening my face to help get a grip on my pose. That produced a facsimile of tension. In yoga, tension is never an asset.

The face doesn't lie unless you tell it to.

In yoga, the look on peoples' faces syncs with the quality of their pose.

If your face works hard to maintain Warrior 3, you'll wobble.

If your face is at rest, your tree pose will exude calm confidence.

Our faces can get caught up in what we're thinking. That inside voice may be telling secrets with a strained jawline. You want to look like what you want to feel.

The face you take out into the world will determine how the world greets you.

For most of my life, my face was tinged with panic.

I telegraphed that I was late. Stressed. Too much to do on the to-do list.

And that's exactly what people sometimes saw.

Now, if I see or sense tension north of my eyebrows, if I feel my brow furrow, I command it to assume an at-ease position.

It works. When tension leaves my face, I feel it inside and out.

Don't let emotion be the boss of you.

Let your face do the talking.

"NOTHINGNESS. CAN YOU GET THERE?"

It's cold. The car seat feels like I'm sitting on frozen meat. I'm bundled up in the cozy embrace of fleece and old, retired cashmere. January days often start out in a cocoon of quiet. I'm winding my way to yoga. I'm reflective. Relaxed. Then, without warning, I encounter a moment of alarming mystery and painful enlightenment—I lock eyes with a lonely, winter-skinny deer. In this sphincter clenching David Fincher moment, the deer sees the twisted depths of my inner soul. She knows I planted a deer-resistant hedge.

Fifteen minutes later I'm on my mat, and I push back into a child's pose. I'm haunted by that deer. How do these animals survive the winter? They all have that ghostlike look of climate refugees you see in a *60 Minutes* story.

My mind replays all the food I ate since Thanksgiving. How many cookies? How many second helpings?

Cheese. Shrimp. Crabcakes.

Does everybody's aunt make fudge?

How many Manhattans have I raised to toast the holidays? I'd be much happier if that deer had gained the ten pounds I accumulated over the past two months.

And class starts.

"Blah, blah, blah about the New Year…a fresh start…the stress of holidays…move your energy in a different direction…less equals more…nothingness. Can you get there?"

Nothingness?

"…Can you get there?"

No. Nothingness? No. Haven't you heard—there's always something!

"Forget your list. Forget the traffic. Let go of work. Forget everything that happened last weekend. Forget what's happening this weekend. Literally, imagine nothing."

Okay—this is not happening. How can I think about nothing when all I'm thinking about is how stupid this sounds knowing that all around us the woods are crying with deer barely able to stand on their own four hooves.

"Nothingness is a treasure chest of physical and emotional benefits."

Nothing is impossible. Wait a minute—isn't that an ad campaign for Adidas? Yeah, that's the line. It's an awesome campaign. And I agree—"nothing" is fucking impossible. There's always something on my mind! Nothingness. That's just bad copy.

Rather than relaxing in the semi-meditative moment that inaugurates every class, which I've finally come to embrace, I'm suddenly irritated by this tea-towel yogism.

I can't even listen to the rest of her blah, blah, blah about nothingness. I idle in neutral until we push back to our first downward dog.

For the next seventy-five minutes, the class is a blur. My mind keeps going back to this idea of nothingness.

I ask myself, *Well if nothingness seems so impossible, what's in the way? What is my mind doing when I'm alone with my thoughts?*

Some old squirrels use my mind like a gym:

- Is my friend _____ really my friend?
- I replay regrets, particularly things I've left unsaid.
- I game-plan my to-do list, which never gets shorter.

After a steady routine of poses, yogi orchestrates a downshift, dimming the lights and music. Stevie Nicks's "Landslide" wafts softly over the room.

"Let's slow it down. Reclaim calm with your breath. Let's head toward nothingness. How do you get rid of the squirrels in your head?"

She can see my squirrels?!

"How do you shut off your mind?"

How do I shut out the picture of that starving deer?

I feel for Bambi, out in the chilly woods alone, trying to find a patch of something even remotely edible. I've never been that hungry. At the worst, I've suffered intense cravings for a pumpkin chocolate scone from Seven Grams in NYC. Guilt makes its move to center stage. The deer, the problems of the world, the angst of the day—they're are all still there.

I'm not sure I'll ever get to nothingness. In fact, that's not such a bad thing. "Nothingness" is a nice concept. An idea. But if you give two shits about anything—the deer, your dog, your family, the less-than-lucky, the planet—"nothingness" in this life is nothing to strive for.

I encourage "somethingness." Melinda Page (the elder) recruited me to work with her on Stockings With Care—a miracle of an organization in NYC that makes Christmas happen for families living in the city's shelters. Imagine, you're a mom with two young kids, waking up in a shelter on Christmas morning. No Santa. No toys. No joy. SWC makes it possible for that same mom to make Christmas come alive for her kids. Thanks to the big heart of Rosalie Joseph and her army of volunteers and donors, thousands of gifts are wrapped and distributed to women in need throughout the city. Mom decides if those gifts are from her or from Santa. For her, it's a gift of empowerment. And that is very real.

Ever since Melinda introduced me to the opportunity to do something that makes a difference in someone's world, "somethingness" has given me the gift of turning my angst into action.

There's a lot to worry about in our world. Through various organizations, my squirrels have been tasked with solving other people's problems.

If you have the time, energy, or money, "somethingness" is a great way to combat futility, fear, and self-doubt. "Something is power." It's a deep well of purpose and connection. If everyone contributed a little "somethingness" somewhere, well, that would be everything.

I get it. Yogi wanted us to a have a clear head. Peace of mind.

"Nothingness." Shavasana for the brain.

But "Nothingness" is an indulgence. A true luxury in a broken world. Without ten milligrams of valium, a gummy bear or Propranolol, "nothingness" is impossible.

I guess you can't believe everything you hear in a yoga class.

"NOTHINGNESS IS MY NEW NEW YEAR'S RESOLUTION!"

Class ends. I'm wet-wiping my yoga blocks.

I am drenched by the positive energy of a bouncy woman, who says to me, "I never thought about it, but nothingness is exactly what I need."

Awkwardly, I have nothing to say.

"Do you have any resolutions?"

"Same as every year. Walk more."

I walk without purpose. I don't treat it like a workout. I don't saddle the walk with a goal or destination or walk in service of chores. There's no goal other than taking a walk. The dog and the phone are left at home, and I just walk.

As I write this, I fear you might imagine me living inside a fluty Kenny-G world.

On the days when I'm giving myself a disappointing year-end review, I start walking. When I'm outside, breathing in the air and light, I feel layers of tension peel away. Walking at a steady pace, the rhythm creates a sense of calm. On most walks, "poor me" gets left behind somewhere around mile three. The stream of regrets recedes, and a trickle of possibilities reveals itself. I step over the threshold into positive space. That's when I can have a productive conversation with the unresolved issues that hide in the heart. At the end of the walk, there are no dragons left to slay, no more battles to win. I'm able to make the calls I don't want to make, accept realities that aren't always ideal, or calmly confront a friend about something shitty they might have said or did the night before yesterday.

My first organized hiking trip was in Norway (spoiler alert: luxury anecdote ahead). One very bleak day, we faced a fourteen-mile trek. It wasn't the most challenging path, but it was made even longer by a relentless rain. This did not match the idyllic, sunny mountaintops and fiords pictured in the *Backroads* brochure. The first few miles were dedicated to cursing the weather and bemoaning how fantastic this hike would be on a sunny day. I felt nothing but wet. Very, very wet.

At some point, I was just walking. I stopped calculating how many miles we had covered. All I could hear was rain. It was purposeful, hitting the ground with solid determination. It became its own white noise, providing a focal point—like a meditation mantra. I'd never walked in the rain before. Maybe I ran from the car to an AMC movie theater. Or bolted down a city block to pick up an overpriced salad. But I'd never just walked in the rain without calculating how to get inside as quickly as possible. Rain was an enemy. After all, isn't rain really bad for your shoes? But hiking shoes—fabricated with wetness in mind—liberate you from that concern.

In that moment, walking through that Norwegian pine forest in the rain, life was different than it had ever been. It would have been equally awesome on a sunny day, but how often do we spend an entire day outside in the rain? I knew then that I would never forget that day. How many days provide such vivid memories? Not just what happened, but also the feel and smell of the memory. At noon, I stood under a tree that cut the rain in half. The sandwich I'd made that morning would be nominated for my top-five favorite meals of all time, not because the sandwich was so amazing, but because the whole experience was something to savor.

In the rush of life during my previous twenty years, how often had I ever really "savored" lunch? Never. Lunch competed with a race against deadlines. But there I was, *loving* a truly uncomfortable day.

I can still feel the transcendence of stepping into a hot shower that evening. That night, I devoured a somewhat average dinner that, in spite of its ordinariness, tasted so damn good. I soaked up the wisdom of that rainy day and never forgot it: Instead of lamenting what you don't have, savor what's in front of you.

I've been a runner for most of my life. I regularly clocked six-, eight-, or ten-mile runs. On some days, I stretched it out to thirteen miles. Oddly, I never did a marathon. I know all about the "runner's high." The emotional lift from walking is different. I know the value of talking things through with friends or therapists. Walking is different. Walking will steer you into a dialogue with yourself. I don't get to set the agenda for the conversation in my head. As I wander, my mind wanders too, going where it needs to go.

The subconscious knows what it really wants. I've been able to resolve the loss of friendships. I've walked through the confusing end of a job or client relationship. I rewrote the story of my father after seeing a bigger context for his cold distance. Instead of seeing a prick, upon walking I saw a man who probably never wanted to have kids. My dad had a gambler's spirit. He loved the track. He owned race horses. It's clear now: He had no interest in playing dad to three boys and three girls. But he was dictated by generational, societal, and Catholic expectations. He had the kids. He provided for the family. Done and done. Play father? No—let the mother do the parenting. Dad was an angry guy. He was trapped by the confines and responsibilities of his parochial life. I've often thought that he resented his own kids because of the freedoms and choices that were open to us. Opportunities he created for us. Options he never had. In some ways, we became strangers to him, living lives in worlds very different from his world.

While walking, I've been able to embrace my dysfunctional family as a strange but essential ingredient of who I've become. My sense of humor developed as I played witness to the absurdities and dramas of my family's dysfunction.

Digression: I can claim a sense of humor. In fact, I have proof. I've been paid by major Hollywood studios to write comedy. Believe me, you can't work with creative executives if you don't have a sense of humor about their farcical notes.

Now, you just said, "Wait a minute, that sounds harsh! He doesn't sound funny, he doesn't sound open, and, in fact, he sounds like sour grapes. And a little bitter. Seems to me he might be the one who's difficult to work with."

If it please the court of public opinion, here's a true story I submit in my own defense:

EXT. DISNEY STUDIOS, BURBANK,
CALIFORNIA – EARLY 1990s

A beautiful day at the Dream Factory. Michael Norton, a thirty-something writer, a recent expat from NY, jumps from his silver Volvo and races toward the entrance of a building adorned with the Seven Dwarfs. Exuding optimistic energy, if Michael was the eighth dwarf, his name would be Zippy.

INT. CONFERENCE ROOM, DISNEY STUDIOS – MOMENTS LATER

Michael sits with his Creative Executive, a woman best-suited to directing customers to the oral care section at a CVS. They are reviewing the first draft of the comedy pilot Disney has hired Norton to write for ABC.

DISNEY EXECUTIVE

There's nothing funny on this page.

MICHAEL

(very confused)

I don't understand.

DISNEY EXECUTIVE

There's no jokes!

MICHAEL

I'm sorry, but…I think there's a couple of laugh-out-loud moments—

DISNEY EXECUTIVE

Where?! I don't see them.

MICHAEL

Well…they're there. I know they're there.

DISNEY EXECUTIVE

Well, maybe you have a different sense of humor—

MICHAEL

(inside voice, worried)

Or maybe you don't have any sense of humor.

DISNEY EXECUTIVE

(seeing the question mark on the writer's face)

Show me. Show me where the jokes are.

Read it to me.

Michael reads from the top of the page. The executive doubles over with laughter. At least five jokes land. They get scores of 9.0 from the imaginary comedy judges. The last one scores a winning 10.0. No laugh track required for this page. It's comedy gold.

DISNEY EXECUTIVE

Well, sure, it's funny if you read it like that.

And scene!

"It's funny if you read it like that." How can you be a comedy executive if you don't understand how comedy works? How can you be a comedy executive if you don't understand that a script is written for actors to act?

On that rain-drenched hike in Norway, I revisited my time at Disney. I made peace with my limited success as a writer in Hollywood, happy for the memories, but no longer mourning the A-list career I never had. For the first time, I saw that leaving LA actually saved me from becoming a smokey, disgruntled writer who spends the greater part of every day "hating the business."

What we've had and what we've *never* had make us who we are. The good and the bad conspire to put us where we're at. For a time, my identity was wrapped around my failure. I was the person who never became who he thought he'd be.

While walking, things get left behind. When I get lost in my regrets, walking helps me find the path back to the present. When walking with others, whether they're friends visiting for the weekend or strangers on a hiking trip, I'm wowed by the stories they share. Walking seems to free people from the limits of polite conversation. Walking provides access to the conversations we really need to have. I've walked with a couple who had lost a child while she was away at camp—a senseless story I had actually seen on the nightly news. It was one of many stories we see in our feeds that prompt fleeting, bite-size heartbreak. Meeting them in real life, I felt the true weight of their story. These digital flashes of horror happen to real people, and their stories last much longer than thirty seconds. I could see this couple "walking it out."

On another trip, I walked with a woman who survived 9/11 because she switched shifts at the Pentagon with a coworker. Her coworker perished, perhaps right where she might have been working had she gone to the office that day. She was "walking it out." So, too, was a guy recovering from the completed suicide of his fiancé.

The most vivid story was that of a sixty-six-year-old woman who lost her husband in her twenties. She had no choice but to push forward, get a degree, get a job, and get all of her four kids through college. This hiking trip in Croatia was her first vacation since she lost her high-school sweetheart over forty years ago.

While walking in deserts, mountains, and along dramatic coastlines, I've listened to people tell their stories. Mile after mile, through tears and smiles, I saw their shoulders lift as they took in more air. I watched faces transform with bits of relief. With each step, they were on their way to some version of acceptance. Of course, one week of hiking doesn't immediately turn every frown upside down, but when the group disbands at the end of a hiking trip, "goodbye" is often paired with "keep walking."

"Keep walking" is also the fantastic brand line of Johnny Walker. Since the campaign's introduction in 1999, that line has sold a lot of scotch. It works because it smartly celebrates what's next for consumers. There is wonder and possibility in the unknown.

You may be thinking, *These hiking trips are fucking depressing!* Not at all—sharing stories is a gold mine of experience and insights. My fellow hikers made me keenly aware that everybody has a story. I now know never to judge people solely by their chitchat and definitely not by my first impression. If I did, I might miss the people I need to meet.

In the physical world and the digital universe, we have all sorts of tools to get us where we want to go. In the emotional world, we don't always see where we need to go. We don't know the road our mind needs to travel. I've found that the simple act of walking has been my greatest tool for navigating the swirl of confusion that too often hijacks my day.

Right now, it is a beautiful day. And that doesn't mean it's sunny and warm. But it's a perfect day for a walk, and, for me, that's always a good day. So, I'm out of here. If you're reading this, you should get going too.

"A FART."

There is wisdom in a yoga fart.

No one wants to be "the farter" in a yoga class, but it happens. It's human and, 99 percent of the time, even the farter is shocked by this break in the silence. No one actively and consciously decides to let one rip when they thrust their butt up into a downward dog.

A public fart in junior high will brand a student for life. If you farted in science class, twenty years later, you'll still be greeted as "stinky," "fartso," or "gasman" at your high school reunion.

As adults, let's not brand anybody "the farter." In yoga and in life, the time will come when that farter is you. Sometimes, it will be a metaphorical fart. A mistake. A foot-in-mouth moment. Whether the misstep is in your personal or professional life, stay calm. The stink will eventually evaporate.

A yoga fart is a great reminder: In whatever you do, seriously commit, but don't get trapped in your seriousness. You do not have control over everything, so learn to expect the unexpected. And of course, when you fart, take the high road and act like it was the person next to you.

"CLOSE YOUR EYES SO YOU'RE NOT COMPARING YOURSELF TO OTHERS IN THE ROOM."

Yeah—well, there's a whole bunch of bending and folding that women do but guys can't.

That's me, talking to me. In the winter, on a Monday morning, it's not unusual for me to be the only guy in the room. I feel my "maleness" in just about every pose. Bulky. Nothing feathery about me. I don't land a pose lightly, I am a *thud* heard around the studio.

Fill in this *Mad Libs*:

When I am __(place / occassion)__, I am the only __(identity)__ in a room filled with __(dominant identity of the majority)__.

Different people feel this difference—oddness, otherness—in different ways and in different circumstances. You may be the only woman in a corporate meeting, the only gay in the village, or the only person of color in a very white grocery store.

When I'm at yoga, it's often my gender and not my sexuality that's my onliness.

I become more hyperaware of me. My sweat. My body hair. The heft of my thighs. My "maleness." I wonder what these women would talk about if I wasn't in the room. Would they be sharing intimacies? Would they be trashing men? Would they be freer? Sillier? More at ease?

I see what they can do with their bodies. I feel my structural limitations that I'll never be able to muscle through. The women seem to have a unique set of physical capabilities and possibilities. I've never seen a guy who could match a woman in a yoga throwdown. Well, maybe one or two, but they're an anomaly. YouTube videos can disprove my assertion, but these ultralimber dudes were probably former dancers or gymnasts, so they put in the ten thousand hours required to do Hanumanasana—the splits pose. In reality, if there was a yoga Super Bowl, women would win it every year.

Guys, if you've never gone to yoga, you should. It's humbling.

Unlike the sports men typically play, women don't come to yoga to win. I never see women competing with each other in the room. No one is getting tackled or taken out. Women don't look for congratulations; they don't high-five after handstands or complicated binds. Collectively, they are more accepting and encouraging. And in that, individually, they seem stronger.

You and I are wondering the same thing right now: *What's the point of this little chapter?*

I'm not sure, other than the realization that there are three components of being okay with who you are: improvement, change, and acceptance. My body is both my asset and my obstacle. I've gotten stronger and more limber, but my binding poses are more wishful thinking than a reality.

Yogi guides us into an inverted lotus pose this morning. "Close your eyes so you're not comparing yourself to others in the room."

My eyes close. Suddenly I feel more connected to my body. I have greater command of where I want to take the pose.

Look inward. You'll see who you can be rather than what you're not.

If you focus on where you haven't gotten to, you'll never see how far you've actually traveled. Close your eyes. If you can't see what others can do, maybe you'll stop seeing your own limitations.

Great advice. Even if an inverted lotus pose is, and always will be, wishful thinking.

"WHEN DOES TIME SLOW DOWN?"

The yogi's hands find prayer position. The fidgeting stops. The room goes quiet. Then she says, "When does time slow down?"

The instructor waits for an answer.

She repeats, "When does time slow down?"

I'm thrown. *Is this a yoga riddle?*

No answers from the class.

"It doesn't."

Her pause is masterful.

She continues when she knows we're ready.

"When we think back to when we were kids, we remember time moving slower. It didn't. A kid's version of *Eat, Pray, Love* is *Snack, Play, Nap*. Kids aren't ever in a rush. Kids don't have money, so options are limited. As adults, we chase more possibilities. There's never enough time to do, go, see, and be everything that catches our eye. But, still, this question gnaws at people. We crave more time even though there's no way of getting more. Time is an absolute. What we crave is relaxation. Body, mind, and spirit at peace. Without it, you're always in competition with time."

Why does it always *feel like she's talking to me about me?!*

"Today, don't do poses. Focus your practice on being in sync with your breath. Don't think about the next move. Pull your mind into the room. Into the moment. Let's make this class feel like we're practicing in molasses."

Her pace was so slow, I couldn't anticipate the next move. If I let my mind drift, I lost the pose. A slower pace invited adjustments to every pose. A soft nudge toward perfection.

As is often said in surfer yoga, "It's the easy hard poses that carry the greatest benefit. Easy poses done the hard way—slowly and exactly."

At the end of class, after the "oms" and "namaste," a fellow yogi incredulously declares, "Oh my god, I thought that class went thirty minutes longer—"

Exactly what the instructor was hoping for.

"We can, with a sharpened awareness, spend time wisely, increasing the nutritional intake as we eat up the time we have left."

That's how time slows down. It's getting back to being a kid and just having one thing to focus on. Building a sand castle. Rigging up a tire swing. Sneaking into *Last Tango in Paris.*

One thing at a time.

Slow and exact.

That how I plan my day. Like they say, "Yoga really begins the minute you leave class."

"DON'T FORCE A POSE."

In my first year of yoga, I'd survey the studio with each move we made, bloating with envy as my fellow yogis were effortlessly suspended in graceful, intricate, and complicated poses. I aspired to those beacons of strength and agility, but I was forced to be realistic. My thighs would always be in the way of certain binds and extensions. I set my sights on mastering yoga Bakasana, more commonly known as crow pose. It looks more advanced than it is, but it demands more of you than the more familiar warrior and triangle poses.

Crow frustrated me. I had the strength, but I didn't have command of my center of gravity. My clumsy attempts dissolved into colossal failures.

"Fuck, fuck, fuck" is not a designated yoga breath.

"Don't force a pose."

That's exactly what she said! Just at the moment I was using every available muscle to jam myself into a spastic-looking crow, the yogi issued her correction.

"Don't force a pose."

She's talking to me, right?

"If you're not there yet, trying too hard might set you back."

She was definitely talking to me.

In business, when people take a moment to correct you, they often use the opportunity to also assert their superiority. Yoga teachers don't do that. There are no points to be scored in the room. No bosses or clients to impress. Yogis float their insights out into the universe with a practiced confidence, knowing that, at the right time, their message will be received. They accept that what they know can't be taught, it can only be shared. In yoga, you are your own teacher. Sure, there's tips and guidance, but only if you allow them into your headspace.

Like friendships, relationships, jobs, and jokes, the good poses—the strong ones—require no effort.

"Don't force a pose."

To be honest, this made no sense to me. Like any seasoned type A, I resisted this axiom. As a runner, I pushed myself to add distance. I fought to cut time from my runs. In my work, I happily pulled all-nighters in pursuit of a winning campaign.

"Don't force a pose" stymied me.

On this one, I know me better than you know me, so, yogi, let's agree to disagree.

Class ended. Phone on.

And there it was—an illuminating tidbit popped up in my news feed. The clouds cleared. A bit of wisdom shined through. Clearly, Siri had been listening. The article announced that it was possible to faint while pooping. You can! Search "vasovagal response" and "defecation response." If you force it or strain too hard to make number two happen, you can pass out while sitting on the crapper. I guess forcing a pose or poop comes with risk.

Imagine what could happen if your face kisses the bathroom tiles. When people ask how you lost your front tooth, what are you going to tell them? Will you open up and tell the truth? Will you turn it into a comedy routine, replaying the crazy faces you made trying to make poop happen? Will you become addicted to colonics—a way to guard against another frightening faceplant?

No more straining! About anything. Don't force the poop. Don't force the pose. Do the work that's required to get from A to Z, safely and surely. Faster doesn't make you better. As I tell my students, "Don't just get it done, make it great."

In yoga, you can't just strike a pose. You have to be authentic in the posture. You earn it with a steady, assured build over time. If you force it, it's always going to be shaky. Nobody wants to be the "wobbler"—the shaky yogi that undermines everyone else's concentration.

One day, when I least expected it, when I wasn't even thinking, I found myself in a side crow. This was my Everest. I'm not sure how or why, but the pose was suddenly available to me.

A flash of recognition: *It's the effortless, at-ease jogs that stretch into your longest runs. The best campaigns write themselves. When you travel, aimless meandering in unknown places often leads you to magical moments.*

I wondered, in the same style David Byrne wondered, *And you may find yourself in a side crow pose on a beautiful day.*

And you may ask yourself, "Well, how did I get here?"

I didn't force it.

I let it happen.

Is *that* the damn key to a happy life?

Sometimes, it's that simple. Sometimes, when you just let life happen, you feel more alive in the moment.

I was always the person who scripted how life was going to go. But when the day, night, career, or plan went off-script, I was the architect of my own disappointment.

"You can't force a pose."

Not too long ago, I would have argued that point with testaments to creative visualization. But now, I know the crow pose only happened when I least expected it. I can't wait to see what else might happen without me getting in the way of it.

"NAMASTE."

As they say…

Truth be told, for a long, long time, I felt stupid saying this at the end of class. Like many people, I never knew what it meant beyond being the official signal that class was finished. If I remember my Catholic past correctly, it's kind of like "Go in peace" at the end of mass.

Coopted by popular culture, "namaste" has become a yoga cliché—a commercialized catchphrase that adorns a vast array of product, including a gluten-free waffle and pancake mix. It's true. You can order it online.

The literal translation is "greetings to you," used as a salutation to a divinity, often speaking to the life force that lives in all of us. Among Hindi speakers, it has become a simple greeting, like "hello."

This little ritual at the end of each class is the totality of religious practice in my life. I like the moment. It's fleeting, but when I'm focused on that moment, it feels like a power-dose of spirituality. Red Bull religion.

When I hear twenty-five voices chanting that one word in unison, in that instant, I often wonder if I am in fact connected to some greater life force. The collective energy produces a moment of belonging. Connectedness. Community.

Whether it's a Sunday service, a Saturday Sabbath, or a simple "namaste" at the end of yoga, there is value in the moments that connect you to yourself and to others.

I've grown to love me my "namaste," as they say, but I never want it on a T-shirt or a coffee mug. Besides, I'm not a T-shirt guy—they make me look old. I need a collar.

If you're going to "namaste," "namaste" like you mean it.

(Hmm...maybe I want *that* T-shirt?)

THE YOGA COOLDOWN

Shooting the shit after class.

"THIS PLACE SHOULD BE A SITCOM."

People say this a lot. Much too often. I've heard it said about ad agencies, hair salons, law offices, art galleries, apartment buildings, Bergdorf Goodman, a pottery studio, an overpriced farmstand, Maybelline's New York offices, CrossFit gyms, SoulCycle classes, and a yoga studio.

No. Sitcoms are character-driven, not place-driven. Places are simply the backdrops for quirky characters to lovingly annoy each other.

I've never had a good laugh at a yoga studio.

Yoga isn't funny.

Art galleries are not funny because art people are not funny. Artists are not driven to entertain us. Art is provocation. No one laughs at an art opening. People smoke. They drink wine. They scowl. At most, you'll get a Mona Lisa smile.

Ad agencies are not funny. Sure, there's always one funny person, but, for the most part, ad people are the waiters of the creative class. They are there to serve up what the client ordered.

They can be clever, but they can also be prickly. When they try to color outside the lines, most of the time, clients smack back. How funny can anybody be when they're always wondering if they might lose the business? And now the entire ad industry is fretting about how the business can compete with the genius and immediacy of AI.

The unfunniest place I've ever worked was Maybelline. There's nothing funny about beauty. Beauty is a fear-based business. I know cosmetics can lift a woman's spirit and self-confidence, but the energy that goes into marketing the stuff is a pretty ugly proposition. All messaging takes an underlying stab at women's psyches. "Without this [insert beauty product here], you'll look old, ugly, tired, lifeless. You won't be cool or stylish. No flirting allowed." There's nothing funny about an industry that creates a world without pores. Real people have real pores. I've been face-to-face with Adriana Lima recording a voiceover. She's shockingly beautiful. She's ridiculously nice. But she has pores. With all the tricks of the trade at work, every model's pics are "enhanced" into false promises.

Sorry, Maybelline, but there's no sitcom lurking in the hallways of your offices. You take your no-clump mascara much too seriously. Beauty isn't a funny business, but it's a business that laughs all the way to the bank.

When yoga people say, "This studio should be a sitcom," I matter-of-factly say, "No, it should only be a sitcom if Julia Louise Dreyfuss or Jean Smart are playing the yoga instructor." Only they could turn a downward dog into a laugh line.

"YOU EAT CHEESE?"

After a Saturday morning class, I duck into Cavaniola's Gourmet for a small round of Kunik cheese and my current obsession—charcoal crackers. Oh my god—I love cheese. And cheese loves me. It hangs with me forever.

As I exit with my little bag of goodies, a woman from class is outside furiously answering a text. She involuntarily glances up, sees me, sees the telltale bag, and demands to know, "You eat cheese?!"

She's surprised. She makes no effort to hide the judgy tone of her question.

"Yes. I eat cheese." In an attempt to assuage my guilt, I offer up a pointless distinction: "Good cheese."

"Lucky for you, you don't look like a cheese-eater."

I'm not advocating weight gain or weight loss, but I know 4 percent body fat is unrealistic. Unless you're a professional ice skater or competitive gymnast, 4 percent body fat is a rolling river of no. Four percent body fat is a waste of cheese occasions.

Weight gain can make you feel older. It slows you down. I don't think there's ever been a man sexier than a young Marlon Brando. Conversely, I'd never want to see old Marlon Brando stepping out of the shower. Marlon gained a shocking amount of weight, rendering him almost unrecognizable. I have photos of hottie Brando and hot-mess Marlon dead center on my mood board. It's the motivation I need to fight the genes of my father. I'm not fat-shaming. I don't think everyone should be held to the Hemsworth standard. In many ways, genes are destiny and age commands its own agenda. The only standard to adhere to is whether you look in the mirror and see the person you want to be.

Most people peak at twenty-eight. That's the year when self-awareness and self-confidence sync with your muscle mass and BMI. You are fierce and focused. You're solid, physically and emotionally. At twenty-eight, you look yummy no matter what you're wearing. After twenty-eight, you have to focus and work hard to hold onto this fleeting moment of you at your best.

I started running in college, back when cheese and crackers were my best friends. There weren't many runners on the road then. Running was the ideal sport for male anorexics. I could run six to ten miles a day and then cheese the night away. To enable my cheese addiction over the years, I've powered through Pilates, yoga, Bikram yoga, weight training, swimming, TRX, and circuit training.

The day comes for all of us, if we're lucky enough to make it there: We blow out fifty candles, and our metabolism hands us its letter of resignation. We swear we'll never go above a thirty-three-inch waist. But we do. We can still run six miles a day, but our knees don't want to. To avoid looking like older Brando, we swear off cheese. We swear off lots of stuff. Our contemporaries adopt an air of superiority around a cheese plate or cookie tray. They seem to say, "Watch me *not* eat this." But we all know that a baby carrot with a dollop of hummus can't compete with a big hunk of aged Manchego on a Raincoast Crisp.

For me, cheese is the root of all evil. I can gain seven pounds over a single weekend without really trying. I now treat cheese as if it's a rationed product, like oranges in wartime England. All I ever want for Christmas is that fired-up metabolism that grants unlimited access to fettuccini alfredo. In the '90s, I embraced *Melrose Place* drag: white T-shirt tucked into my jeans, topped off with a black leather jacket.

Tucked-in shirt! I haven't done that in over a decade!

I don't want to turn into the FatBooth version of me, but life's too short to live forever in a no zone.

I reconciled my relationship with cheese in a spreadsheet. A hard no is impossible, but too much yes can cost you your wardrobe. That can be painfully expensive.

So the question is: To cheese or not to cheese?

Here's the test:

1. Do you look good in a bathing suit without sucking in that little tummy roll?
    a. If yes—eat the cheese.
    b. If no—find another bathing suit and swim more laps.
2. Do you put cheese on your salad and vegetables?
    a. If yes—don't. Cheese is not an ingredient, it is its own food group best enjoyed on a cracker.
    b. If "Who the fuck cares?" is your answer, then cheese on, dude! Besides, a beefy mix of a rebellious confidence can be wildly attractive.

If you're a body fat 4-percenter, you are tight and ripped. You look amazing. There isn't a pair of Mr. Turk pants that aren't perfect for you. It's probably a combination of hard work and impressive discipline. If a single-digit body fat percentage is natural to you, you won the gene pool. Whether you're 4 percent, 10 percent, or 26 percent body fat, the real you can get lost in the terror of self-consciousness. You're not at your best if you're living in a world of no. A no person is never at ease.

No requires determination, but it can blunt the joy of who you are.

With just about everything, learning to live a yes life makes you more interesting than being stuck in the no lane.

So, unless you're competing for the gold in 2028, now and then, say yes to a little cheese.

And I do. Cavianola's is an easy stop on the way home from yoga. It's where I discovered those small rounds of Kunik, charcoal crackers and homemade dark chocolate peanut butter cups. Occasional indulgence is an additional benefit of a dedicated yoga practice.

"THEY DRIVE ME CRAZY."

Class ends. As I walk out onto the streets of Chelsea, I overhear this whispered exchange.

"I want to say something, but then I become the negative one in the room."

"Who are you talking about, camel-toe or ball-sack?"

"No, the Madame Dharma."

I love the bitchiness I'm hearing. I do miss the city sometimes.

"Dharma" refers to the natural order of things. In yoga, it gets closer to your personal path, the duty and order you bring to your life. Your dharma is your true self.

On the few occasions I've visited this studio, Madame Dharma always disrupts the natural order of the room. They consistently show up five minutes late, drowning in their own drama. They sweep in with bags, bottles, and blankets, pretending no one can hear them. Of course, five people need to shift their mats to make room for this frazzle-dazzler. Sure, now and then, we all have good reasons for being late, but when it's your norm, traffic isn't the problem, it's you—you're the problem.

Back to the aforementioned camel-toes and ball-sacks.

You can't believe the shit I've seen at yoga. One thing I learned pushing back to downward dog is that I do not envy the life of a dermatologist, proctologist, or gynecologist. If you're going to thrust your ass up and back toward someone's face, kindly manage your junk. A sport brief is a good gift to give yourself.

"HEY, BUDDY—YOU KNOW WHERE TO GET MY PHONE FIXED?"

I'm headed to my car, yoga mat under my arm. I wasn't happy with today's class. There's been a string of guests at the house. Too much cheese. Too much pie. More wine than usual. I can feel it in the twists and binds. A little unsettled in the standing poses. I know—"It's not a competition." Unless you have a class where you suck.

"Hey, buddy—you know where to get my phone fixed?"

Young guy. Young dude, actually. He's got that just-off-the-beach look. Benson Boone eyes. I look around. There's nobody but me. I guess I'm "buddy."

"Sag Harbor. There's a store—"

"I don't want to drive to Sag."

"That's all I got—"

"Hey—can I just use your phone? For like a minute."

A fog of weirdness just rolled in.

"My girlfriend—she's pregnant—I'm supposed to pick her up but my car's down at the beach. I think the battery died...."

"And your phone's not working?"

"Fucking wave came up while I was out on my board."

"So you can't drive to Sag anyway?"

"Right! I have to hitch unless you're headed that way."

"So, you want to get your phone fixed before you get your car fixed?"

"I asked, like, a hundred people. Nobody has jumper cables."

"But what about your girlfriend?" *Why am I having this conversation?* I know we're on the road to crazy town.

"No phone. I can't Uber. I'm going to have to cab it. You're so right, I got to get to a fucking cash machine."

I didn't say anything about a cash machine.

"What time is it, anyway?"

"Eleven forty-five."

"Dude, I can tell you're a good guy. Do you have, like, twenty-five bucks? I can Venmo you."

"You don't have a phone."

"Later! I can fucking Venmo you later!"

"I got to go. Good luck, okay."

I do not head to my car.

"Jesus, what's fucking forty bucks to you anyway? You're fucking taking yoga. Trust me, poor people don't do yoga."

Coffee shops are safe spaces. I start heading in the direction of a latte.

"Fuck it all, man. If I were you, I'd just give me fifty bucks and say have a nice day. Fucking prick."

"How many times a day do you do this routine? You don't even have a girlfriend."

"I have a girlfriend."

"No, you don't. And your car's not broken down. Your phone is probably muted."

"I have a girlfriend. She's so over me, though. Okay—look—she's mid-Island, and I'm, like, five miles from empty. I need gas, so, like, fifty bucks would do it."

He tries a stare down, but he lacks conviction. This gives me a moment to admire the tightness of his jawline and the sharpness of his features. I realize all of my friends now have big ears.

"Look, it's her birthday."

"There's no future in working this scam. You're working with an old business model. Nobody has cash anymore."

"I know. Fucking debit cards and Venmo!"

I arrive outside Jack's Coffee.

"You going in there?"

"I suppose you want a coffee?"

"Oh jeez—no—I'm caffeine-free just a little over a year. But I really love their apple cider donut."

"If I buy you a donut will you leave me alone?"

"Deal."

Yoga works. And doesn't work.

Before yoga, I wasn't approachable. I wore the face of a preoccupied, stressed out, always-ten-minutes-late marketing guy. The crazies didn't even try to get my attention. I looked crazier than they did. No way was I slowing down for even five seconds of their psychotic non sequiturs. Tourists never asked for directions. Street scammers knew I'd laugh at their bullshit.

Suddenly, I'm the guy every tourist stops. No matter where I am, scammers single me out of the crowd, and the crazies seem to think I'll understand their rants. Is street-screed an established language? I really hope the crazies understand each other when they cross paths. I hope so. Since the government abandoned them and most people ignore them, it would be nice to know they at least have each other.

After decades of navigating the streets and subways in the peace and quiet of anonymity, suddenly I must look like I'm visiting from Oklahoma.

It's the yoga.

I move at a slower pace. I must appear open and accessible. It's the downside of the new me – the calm me. People talk to me. Sometimes it's incomprehensible. Sometimes it's funny. Odd. Intrusive. My favorite are the cons that start with flattery:

"You look like a goddamned movie star." (Good sunglasses can do that for you.)

"Man knows how to pick out a tie!"

"Now that's a sweater!" Whoever just said that knows her audience. My sweaters are my children. "It's a really nice weave."

I meet the eyes of a young woman. They sparkle in a color between green and blue. She is crouched against the relentless concrete of an FIT building just off Seventh Avenue.

"You have great sweaters."

She's seen me before, and yet I've never noticed her. Not even once. My eyes are owned by my phone. She smiles, but just barely. Just enough so I can see who she is. Or used to be.

She is right. My sweater has a great weave. It is a chunky black turtleneck from John Varvatos's first collection. It has a ribbed weave that gives it texture and a structured fit. Its "extraness" always signals relaxed luxury. This is a when-in-doubt sweater. This sweater goes wherever it needs to go. I've been wearing it for twenty years, and it always looks new and now.

I could write a hundred stories about who this young woman might have been before her metaphorical fall. And before she could get up, she fell between the cracks.

I am just three blocks from home.

Sometimes, the immediacy of a moment runs faster than all other instincts. Would she wear it? Would she sell it? Do I have the time to run back home for a change of sweater?

I'm not on a deadline. In fact, I am headed to a meeting with a client who is always late, and, by that, I mean hung over and snarly.

Here I am again, caught in this new headspace between guilt and gratitude for everything I have. I will not tell you how many black, blue, and gray sweaters I own. In this moment, I know I own too many. I race home and put on another black turtleneck.

I return to the scene of the compliment. I offer the sweater to my admirer. Like lightning, you can see the excitement race through her body.

No more words need to be exchanged.

The next morning, I'm hurrying up Seventh Avenue when I hear, "Hey, I never said thanks."

There she is, scrunched up inside the black turtleneck.

"Looks good on you."

"Looks good on anybody, I bet."

She's right about that. A good sweater always looks good.

I never see her again.

I've always wondered where that sweater may have gone.

Did it remind her of who she used to be?

Did she reclaim the life she once lived?

Did she go back to her family in Idaho or Vermont or Ohio?

Was the sweater stolen from her in a shelter?

Did she pass it on to someone else?

So yeah—it's the yoga. I'm calmer. More approachable. People talk to me. Sometimes, it's a disturbing intrusion. A verbal assault. A situation for which I have no contribution or solution. But sometimes, it's a conversation that could only be fated to happen.

If you know me, you might be thinking, "He's sounding a little twee. I thought this book was going to be a bitchy cut on the Hamptons." If you don't know me after 143 pages, you may be thinking, *Who is this privileged twee poser with oniomania?*, which the dictionary defines as "an obsessive or uncontrollable urge to buy things." In my case, sweaters.

"I like your sweater" didn't change my life. I doubt it changed much in the life of that young woman. But in that small, isolated, and somewhat insignificant exchange, her day and my day levitated momentarily.

I'm pulling myself back from the temptation to get preachy, but it's easier to dehumanize the needy than it is to face their reality. You don't need me to lecture you, but we've been programmed to answer the cosmic call for kindness with digital outrage.

When I think about that moment outside FIT, I wonder, *Did John Varvatos ever walk past her and recognize his sweater?*

New York is weird like that. It's a huge place, but a small world. And then I wonder, *If I hadn't taken up yoga, would I have even seen that woman, or just walked past another person sentenced to life on the streets?*

Impossible to know, but I start thinking bigger.

If the whole world did yoga, would we all see and hear each other with more clarity? Would we respond rather than react to the people who have fallen and can't get up?

"MOM FUCKED UP YOGA."

It's ridiculous what people will pay for a peach. It's even more absurd what they'll pay for a peach-raspberry pie. It doesn't matter here at trust-fund farmstand; the line is as long as a Marc Jacobs sample sale.

Farmstands in the Hamptons are like going to church. Customers behave themselves. Conversations are tinted in hush tones. Phones are nervously silent. You do not annoy the women who rule these joints; one false move, and you could be banished from this Eden of prepared foods.

I'm here with two friends who are visiting for the weekend. They're in the 4 percent club—that's not their income, it's their body fat percentage. I assume they like me because they live vicariously through my portion sizes. I took them to a class designed for surfers; it has a boot camp quality. They're very happy with the calculated calorie burn.

Waiting in line to score a pie for dinner, we're surrounded by fresh-baked porn. The boys are a bit woozy. They imagine a time machine that would whisk us all back twenty years to a much more robust metabolism.

Four blonde college coeds in supercute athleisure wear enter. They were also at surfer yoga. They've got that Erewhon-smoothie look: long straight hair, leggings, bra tops, polar-white sneakers, and clean-girl makeup. They move as one unit; you can't tell where one ends and the other begins. If you know dance, they look like a Pilobolus poster. I look to see if they are, in fact, joined at the hip.

INT. OVERPRICED FARMSTAND - TIME FOR LUNCH

After a sweep of the store, there is a collective gasp; they're eyeing the bikini muffins.

BLONDE

They look exactly like what I want right now.

DIRTY BLONDE

You should get one. You did an amazing class.

BLONDE

I haven't had a muffin in, like, forever.

NATURAL BLONDE

Bikini muffins. What's that mean?

DIRTY BLONDE

Should we split one?

BLONDE

All four of us! We should!

NATURAL BLONDE

I love that.

An ATTENDANT replenishes the shelves. In a town where no one admits to eating baked goods, the farmstand sure does move mountains of muffins.

NATURAL BLONDE

Excuse me, can we just get one muffin?

ATTENDANT

Nope. Just the packages of four.

DIRTY BLONDE

We just want one.

ATTENDANT

For four of you? You girls need to eat.

BLONDE

That's funny! You sound just like my mom!

The moment is hijacked by a voice bellowing into a phone. A BRO has entered the store.

BRO

Nah, my mom fucked up yoga.

BRO'S MOM follows her prince into the store.

BRO

She didn't reserve spots in time. Totally sucks.

BRO'S MOM

What's the salad you like?

BRO

I don't know. You don't remember? You bought it.

BRO'S MOM

I buy everything, but I don't track who eats what.

BRO

Now Mom just fucked up lunch.

ATTENDANT

Hey—you don't talk like that in here, and you definitely don't talk about your mom like that.

BRO

Why are you even listening to my conversation?

ATTENDANT

Hey, junior, see the door? Out you go.

BRO

What? You can't—

BRO'S MOM

He's sorry.

BRO

Sorry for what?

ATTENDANT

For starters, how about sorry for being you.

Bro puffs himself up, considers a moment of defiance, but finds a line of smirking faces staring him down. Mom puts up a defiant hand as if to say, "Fool, think fast, or we'll never get these salted caramel chocolate chip cookies ever again."

Bro skulks toward the exit.

EXT. FARMSTAND – A WHILE LATER

And then there's STANLEY. I only know Stanley's name because as we exit with $187 worth of farm-to-table lunches, the WOMAN working the produce calls out to him as he hobbles out of his Bentley.

WOMAN

How you doing, Stanley? New car!

STANLEY

Got this one to match my wife's eyes.

WOMAN

Lucky lady.

STANLEY

Now she wants another one for Florida. Eh. You got my shrimp?

WOMAN

It's in the back. That's a lot of shrimp.

STANLEY

Eh. You got my pies?

WOMAN

That's a lot of pies. You having a party?

STANLEY

We got the grandkids.

WOMAN

Those are lucky kids.

STANLEY

This is the problem with big houses. It's like I'm running a restaurant. Summer—it's never easy, am I right?

WOMAN

Never has been.

STANLEY

Just trying to get through the weekend.

WOMAN

Aren't we all? Aren't we all?

The woman appears to think to herself, Not lucky like you. Stanley starts picking at tomatoes as if he knows how to pick one.

MY FRIEND

I didn't know Bentleys came in that color.

ME

Why would you?

MY FRIEND

It's my one-day car.

ME

Stop. If you win the lottery, you're going to be driving around in a Bentley?

MY FRIEND

No. I'll be driven around in a Bentley.

OTHER FRIEND

Eeeeew!

MY FRIEND

Don't "eeeeew" me!

ME

A Bentley. You work for a nonprofit?

MY FRIEND

That doesn't mean I can't want nice things.

ME

I just...this is…sorry…I've never seen this side of you.

OTHER FRIEND

You didn't even have a cashmere sweater until you found one at Housing Works.

ME

Wait—you fly one-stop to LA to save, like, fifty bucks. And you dream about having a Bentley?

MY FRIEND

Given the opportunity, we're all a little J. Lo. If I have a Bentley, I probably have everything else.

Point taken.
SCENE.
THE END.

If my friend is trying to manifest a Bentley, he may be immune to the level-setting, consciousness-raising, and attitude adjustments that come with a dedicated yoga practice. He's just in it for the physical benefits, of which there are many.

No judgements. That's another benefit of yoga for me. It's fun to observe life without any need to judge it.

For instance, Bro needs yoga to calm the fuck down so his coworkers in digital marketing, finance, or a tech startup won't have to absorb one more asshole. His mom could use yoga to escape the spoiled, useless monster she created.

And if Stanley, who has Bentley money, finds it tough getting through a summer weekend, then he might benefit from a little yoga with a side of a sound bath.

"WHAT'S NEW?"

Yoga friends. You see them once or twice a week. You know enough about each other to chat for five minutes. It's a nice connection. Nothing deep, but comforting in the familiarity.

Then there's Jim. All the enthusiasm of a puppy. As I roll up my mat after class, Jim bounds over with the same question: "Hey, what's new?"

I can't control my irritation. "For god's sake, nothing's ever new!"

"Nothing at all?"

"Nothing of interest, anyway."

"Ever?"

"Well, what's new with you?"

"I don't know. Nothing…really."

"Exactly."

When your life is shifting, "What's new?" is an irritation. Possibly your most dreaded question. We are not guests on talk shows prepped with key talking points carefully crafted to promote a new movie. Our daily routines are rarely newsworthy. Most people's lives follow a familiar track at a steady pace, which is not a bad thing. Unfortunately, "same-old, same-old" immediately flattens a conversation.

I called my friend Laura one day when she was still living in Madison, Wisconsin. Before she moved to New Mexico. Before she left advertising. Before she gave herself permission to become a painter.

Laura's more than a friend. She feels like the other half of me. We were partners at the Arnell Group. There's never been an easier, happier, more productive, or more prolific collaboration in my life. I endured the day-to-day insanity of the New York office while Laura worked remotely from Madison. This was BZ—Before Zoom—so we worked ear-to-ear on the phone for hours every day. On the occasion of a major presentation, Laura came to New York to work onsite for a few days. When working face-to-face, we had a weird energy. We stumbled over each other's faces. We'd look for approval in each other's eyes. We'd often interpret our "thinking faces" for disagreement. We heard each other more clearly when we didn't see each other.

Laura has her own brand of creativity; her brain has one gear: drive. It's all forward motion. No angst. No petulance. Laura's mind works like a Roomba, constantly sweeping every corner of her brain, which is why her ideas always get better and sharper. She tackles everything like she doesn't know anything, so she's always bursting with something unique—an energizing discovery. Laura has an aha moment every day. Creatively, "aha!" is renewable energy.

Last year, I called Laura to catch up. As with most conversations, I threw out the obligatory "what's new?"

ME: What's new?

LAURA: Tim [the lawyer husband] just joined a firm in Denver with an office in Santa Fe. Our youngest is off to college, so we're selling our house in Madison and buying a new house in Tesuque [wherever that is]. You have to come visit!

ME: New job. New house. New city. Fuck you for having news.

There are stretches in life when you don't have a lot of news. The established routine just extends itself week after week. It startles me when anyone has something to report that isn't about their parents or their kids. It seems so routine and mundane that you get bored with yourself. When people have the audacity to ask "what's new?", it's a tragic reminder that, most days, life just grinds on—stuck in neutral with a view that never changes.

We live in a world powered by "new." Fashion brands are really good at the "what's new?" question. It's essential to their survival. "Pleats. No pleats. Wide leg. Skinny leg. Short. Long. Desert hues is all you need." Similarly, mobile phone sales are generated by the steady stream of advanced features. Camera. Megapixel. Multishot. Flash. Timer. Zoom. Filters. Video. You, too, can make a movie. The automotive industry is driven by an annual release of new models. Can you imagine commuting without a cup holder, heated seats, parking assist, fully loaded infotainment and voice-activated connectivity? Without the lure of a shiny new *something*, even a hot brand can quickly become old news.

On the first of the month, ask yourself, "What's new?" If you don't have a good answer, then get busy with something you've never done before.

You might push back. "Don't they say, 'no news is good news'?"

"Yes, they say that, but they're mostly referring to the possibility of disaster. We're in search of good news."

In the months ahead, I could answer that question with, "Well, I'm working on my first book." But I won't. If I don't finish this book or it generates no interest, this endeavor will start to smell like rotting fish. I don't want to navigate my day anticipating and dreading the question, "How's the book going?"

Whether you're twenty-five, thirty-five, or sixty-five, without "new," everything about you gets old.

"New" is forward motion. "New" generates energy and interest. "New" is the gateway drug to the next level of you—the "new" idea of you.

"New" isn't easy. But you knew that.

"YOU KNOW THAT'S A CRAZY PRICE FOR A LOAF OF BREAD."

I often stop at Carissa's the Bakery after yoga; the bliss of "namaste" lasts longer with a chocolate croissant.

I place my order, which includes a loaf of her pickle bread.

I'm startled by the whisper in my ear. "You know that's a crazy price for a loaf of bread."

I spin to meet the smiling gaze of my yogi.

I challenge her, "Well, you're here too."

"Special occasion. Birthday cake."

"You know that's a crazy price for a birthday cake."

"It's Mom. You can't put a price on Mom."

If you live with anything too long, it becomes your new normal.

Neck pain.

Budget-blasting rent.

The price of that fresh-baked bread you can't stop eating.

Yogi's right, though. I've forgotten: My normal isn't normal.

I've been perched on a bar stool at Craft feeling like I've done okay in life, then suddenly I overhear, "I'm good. I feel fresh. I was in first on Emirates, so I took a shower before we landed."

I know from Emirates Airlines commercials that Jennifer Aniston enjoys her showers in the sky, but I always thought, *Who really does that?* I know Jen also hawks dry-eye solutions and Smartwater, but is she *that* busy that she didn't have time to shower before heading to the airport? I assume she's not making the bed and taking out the garbage before she calls for an Uber to catch her flight to Dubai.

I know I'm not poor. But it's all relative. In East Hampton, I feel poor every time I window shop at Compass Realty on Main Street. And I still find it astonishing what people pay for a single peach at a farmstand. I know I've mentioned peach prices before, but seriously, with summer traffic, the peach mafia knows you're not going to drive around to comparison shop.

I need to get out of my bubble.

I've thought this many times. Now and then, I'm repulsed by everything I've grown to love. Or think I need. Or come to expect. Avocado toasts. Japanese Scotches. Eighth-row seats at Brandi Carlisle. I pay the tailor to shorten my dog's coats—my big-boned girl needs the width of a larger size.

My indulgent wish list was constantly replenished by the pages of *Departures Magazine*. Sadly, but thankfully, the magazine printed its final issue in 2021. *Departures* was like an injection of persuasion. For a brief moment once, I wanted this exquisite set of golf clubs…and I don't golf. Yes, I know—I have the luxury of having silly thoughts.

That's why I love a cul-de-sac life. Conceptually. A cul-de-sac protects you from the simmering envy of someone else's much greener grass.

Marketing introduces me to a lot of research. Some you do yourself. Some you subscribe to. Some comes to you thanks to the industriousness of planners. Planners are people who enthusiastically, creatively, and often rabidly immerse themselves in the needs, motivations, and desires of consumers. They study trends. They absorb culture like thirsty sponges. Research makes you sound smarter than you really are. A good planner can make you sound brilliant.

I'm not a research expert; I'm more of a blah-blah-blah person. I don't always remember the source or precise details, but you can depend on me for the gist of it.

At some point, I read some stuff about the happiness quotient of people living in cul-de-sacs. Typically, a cul-de-sac is populated with people just like you. The houses are similar in style, size, and value.

People have similar incomes and acquire a lot of the same stuff. The "sameness" of lifestyle makes it so much easier to think, *I'm doing okay.* People in cul-de-sacs don't spend their day seeing someone else's "more"—they see a paved circle of validation.

Sure, everybody wishes they were doing better, but it only becomes a gaping, festering sore when someone you know actually *does* better. *Or is that just me?* I've met a few people who seem perfectly content with their lot in life. They are the luckiest people I know.

Even cul-de-sacs in East Hampton offer their own unique comfort of sameness. There's a cul-de-sac in the Georgica area of East Hampton that's lined with multimillion-dollar homes, each one nestled into million-dollar landscaping. There are swimming pools and tennis courts, a wardrobe of cars, and a parade of hired help. There's no reason they shouldn't all be ridiculously happy. But let's say one of them was able to put in a heliport. I bet within one gilded season every house in that cul-de-sac would be chopper-ready. On Thursday evenings in August, the swarm of helicopters would be akin to the "Ride of the Valkyries" scene in *Apocalypse Now*. But for now, there is a manicured contentment in the neighborhood.

The cast of *Friends* invented cul-de-sac contract negotiations in 2002. They stuck together like best friends should. Each of the six actors signed a deal for $1 million per episode and NBC's top-rated show stayed on the air for two more seasons. Imagine if Rachel suddenly had much nicer things than Monica. What if Joey had a sweeter deal than Ross and Chandler? That would have been the end of those friendships—onscreen and off!

No matter where I've been in my adult life, there have been people with more and people with less. I seesaw between resentful and grateful. Imagining more keeps me dreaming. Needing more compromises my gratitude.

I know, I know—sometimes I sound like a weightless, glassy-eyed guy who lives on nuts, berries, and essential oils. But when you boil this stuff down to its essence, the truth gets a little spiritual at the core. Our personal values are not an external expression of identity, they are the internal North Star.

Here's a quick exercise: I want you to be the casting director of your ideal cul-de-sac.

Imagine waking up to a bright, sunny day.

You step outside to get the paper. (I know you get your news on your phone, but play along and pretend we're still in an analog world.)

You step outside without any concern for your bedhead or saggy pajama bottoms. Your neighbors are all outside, mowing lawns, getting mail, power walking, throwing frisbees with their dog.

Who do you want to see living in your cul-de-sac?

Who are you always happy to see?

Who makes you comfortable just being you?

Who makes you think, *This is where I want to be!*

It's a simple exercise, informed by internal rather than external stimuli. Looking for your cul-de-sac is not searching through real estate websites and lusting after dream homes—that's just an exercise in frustration. Instead, you'll find greater reward imagining the neighbors who will make your house feel like home. It's how I found Camden, Maine. I've never been there, but it's on my list of places I might like to live if I ever tire of my current life. Camden revealed itself to me through a random search of hiking trails. It seemed to be the epicenter of some inspiring scenery. I "exploogled" images of the town. Charming. It's where they shot the movie *Peyton Place*. Who wouldn't want to live there? I got lost in the fantasy of what it would be like to wake up every day in Camden. I thought about who my new friends might be. They wore jeans, boots, and sweaters. They were big readers and found no shame in pastry.

In that escape to another version of my life, I felt some things that I was craving in my current life. In that small town, my days would be filled with rituals. A set night for Rummikub. Another night for cards or mahjong. Five-mile runs with my best bud. Eight-mile hikes with a posse I met at the coffee shop. There'd be sunset paddles out in the water—solo. Friday-night martinis at the fancy inn on the hill; a chirpy table of New York expats bitching about everything. I fantasized about the breakfast spot where you'd find me on most mornings. I'd have my usual spot in a booth. Lots of easy conversation. The embrace of community. You know, that place "where everybody knows my name." Yes, it would be like *Cheers*—but with pancakes.

I have a short list of small towns and urban neighborhoods that inspire me to imagine a different version of who I am. This is more than a debate about town versus country. It's looking beyond the physical context of living in a new place—it's me needing a new emotional context for how I spend my days. Whether or not I ever change zip codes, it helps me understand what I want to feel in my current life.

I know if my life were to shift to a small town too far from a big city, I'll feel isolated.

If everybody knows my name, I'll miss meeting new people.

The value of this exercise can be unexpected. I'm not in the wrong place; I simply lack the rituals that create my sense of belonging. That I can do. Yoga has given me a place where people know my name.

Yoga also taught me the right questions to ask myself. Yes—it's a crazy price for a loaf of bread, but for me, I want my carbs to be top-shelf.

"HAVE YOU EVER DONE YOUR BRAND SHIT ON YOURSELF?"

This one threw me. I'm staring into the eyes of a woman who really wants to know.

"No. Why would I do that?"

"I don't know. Don't you ever get tired of yourself?"

Of course, I do, but I'm not telling her that. I rummage through my stuff in search of my banana.

"And don't you get the feeling people get tired of you sometimes?"

Okay, she's one of those people—she's never known a boundary she wouldn't cross. She was a little bit threatening, as if raised by a con man.

"I know I left the house with a banana...."

"Oh. Sorry. I didn't know that was your banana. I was hungry."

My inside voice sheepishly squeaks, *But she knew it was somebody's banana. At the very least, she knew it wasn't her banana. It's not like we're in a Days Inn breakfast room.*

"I bet there's a business helping people figure out their shit."

"Well, there is. It's called therapy."

"Yeah...but that don't always work for everybody. I wish I was like Disney. Everybody likes Disney. But I'm not like Disney. I bet you ain't either."

Inside voice: *A little aggressive. Judgmental. Super creepy. Sketchy grammar. I don't want her to know which car is mine.*

"That banana was pretty soft. I'm not a fan of soft bananas."

Oh, Yelp reviews are her blood sport. I counter, "They're good for banana bread."

"I don't bake. Anyway, I took an online quicky quiz to find out what animal I'm most like. Mosquito. It said I'm a mosquito. Nobody wants to be a mosquito. But…I can see how it came out that way."

"Yeah, well, we are who we are."

"But that's why I need a new brand."

Inside voice again: *Hmm…is that something I should do? She's got a point. Branding is like therapy for business. Maybe she's crazy in a prophetic way.*

In my class at Parsons, I lecture about the rise of the human brand. Martha. Oprah. Elon. Addison Rae. Ryan Murphy. Michelle Phan. Tyler Perry. Shonda Rhimes. Kardashians. Joe Rogan. Emma Chamberlain. As our digital connections replace human interaction, we place more value on the people who help us create our best lives. When people find out I'm a "brand guy," anyone with more than a hundred followers on Instagram is suddenly curious about my take on their personal brand.

Yes, to some extent, we are all brands. People are products that hopefully have some use and appeal to friends, mates, and employers. Personally, and professionally, people either buy us, or they don't.

Let's ask the basic question: At its core, what is a brand?

There are many definitions, but this is one of the best:

> **"YOUR BRAND IS WHAT OTHER PEOPLE SAY ABOUT YOU WHEN YOU'RE NOT IN THE ROOM."**
>
> **—Jeff Bezos**
>
> **The guy who made ridiculous amounts of money selling books and reinventing consumerism.**

I start wondering, *What do people say about me when I'm not in the room?* I ask myself this question over and over again.

You can't advise a brand about their business strategy until you understand the role the product plays in people's lives.

What is the role I play in other people's lives?

We either add something to someone's story, or we don't. Our value and relevance can shift. Our needs and wants can also evolve.

When I first moved to LA, I went to a party. I didn't know how to read the room yet.

"Nancy said you just moved here?"

"Yep. Like three weeks ago."

"Actor?"

"No—writer."

"Oh." (Subtext: nothing more pathetic than a struggling writer.)

"I know. We're the busboys of Hollywood."

"Do I know anything you've written?"

"Only if you were an avid troll of off-off-Broadway."

"The hardest thing is getting an agent."

"I have an agent."

"Oh." (A pause. A shift.)

"It's why I moved here. Wanted to be able to give it a real shot."

"An agent at a real agency?"

"I guess. Some guy at CAA." (Game changer. In an instant, I'm either more interesting or more attractive. Or both.)

"Oh. So, you're, like, a *real* writer?" (There's nothing more beautiful than watching the face of a pompous ass flush with envy.)

And that is a sixty-second brand transformation: moving from sad hopeful to a possible contender.

Right now, I often feel like that struggling writer, living with an idea of who I might become. I know this feeling. I played it out when I moved to New York. It was the same when I moved to Santa Monica. And then again with the return to New York. Every move—every change—raises the same question: Who are people going to meet when they meet me next year?

When I was younger, my dream gave me my answer.

As I got older, my fears began to write my story.

That's sort of where I'm at as I write this book.

I took some cues from the yoga studio. I liked the vibe of the people. They were a new breed to me. Not as performative. They didn't show you they were funny. They didn't need to be loved.

"So have you?"

Oh, her! The banana thief. She's still there, staring at me, demanding to know. She's attacking a hunk of cheese, which I assume she had in her jacket pocket. I'm sure my face registers the question, *Wait, if she had cheese, why did she eat my banana?*

I regroup. "Have I ever done the brand shit on myself?"

"Yeah—have you?"

"No. That would be like a dentist drilling his own teeth."

I take my leave. Beelining for my car, I'm already pondering the idea.

What do people say about me when I'm not in the room?

The squirrels in my head are very, very busy.

Isn't it amazing how a total stranger can just fuck up your day?

That woman's intrusive assault on my post-yoga zen was its own lesson. Oddly, I found inspiration in her craziness.

Yes—she is like an annoying mosquito, but she's also weirdly confident. Fearless. Matter-of-fact. Actively in search of who she needs to become.

In yoga, you can't just hop into poses. The details of posture and placement are critical. Life is like that too. You can't just hop into a new identity. A new way of being. Much like a yoga practice, your personal brand's strength is found in the details, built around your core and fully realized through exploration. Maybe this is just a reminder that slow and steady wins the race.

I start my car. I face myself in the rearview mirror.

I haven't done that brand shit on myself. But yoga's changing who I am.

"DO SOMETHING THAT SCARES YOU."

Best advice *ever*!

I'm at Jack's again having a post-yoga coffee. No ticking clock. Just me and my coffee.

Two loud-talkers confab behind me. My phone serves as camouflage so they don't suspect I'm all ears on their conversation.

"You're out of a job every eighteen months."

"You don't have to remind me."

"Look, you want bullshit or honest advice…?"

"Good. Great. Go for it."

Restaurants should have a section for loud talkers.

"By the way, I want your scarf."

"Paul Smith."

"Right. The stripes. Look, you've been doing this shit for twenty-five years. Every time there's a management shift, you guys in the middle are out the door. You know why?

"No one values experience—"

"Nope. You're not fresh. Experience dulls the edge. You appear bored. Is the scarf new?"

"It's, like, three years old. Here, take it."

"The stripes are good, but maybe getting a little played out."

"Just take it."

"I'm good. I don't want it."

"Yeah—you do."

"You can have mine."

"I don't want your scarf."

"Why? It's Loro Piana."

"It's just a gray fucking scarf you paid way too much money for."

"You want another cup of coffee?"

"The only thing I want right now is a career that works."

"Do something that scares you."

"Like what? Skydive?"

"No. Get out of advertising. Go be a freshman in any other business. Do-or-die energy will give you edge. Edge gives you relevance. Relevance is youthful power."

That guy is a dick, but he gives good advice.

I get it: Eventually, you get to a place in your career where there are very few challenges in your work. You've been in the same meeting over two hundred times. You've got the answers. You know exactly what needs to be done in just about any situation.

You don't need another job; it's time for you to do something new. Something that scares you. A challenge that presents a minefield of unknowns. Imagine: Your input can't rely on autofill. You must engage all of your energy and sharpen your focus to even feign competency.

It's good to feel like a freshman again. A little bit of fear prompts a slight buzz. The need to really concentrate is energizing. You have no choice but to caffeinate and overprepare because failure is not an option. You haven't felt like this since the beginning of your career. Yes—that's the feeling you need. Urgency. Vitality. A fun little whip of uncertainty. Like the thrill of a first kiss. Your first time on skis. Putting that little candy-colored tab of heaven on your tongue and riding the drug-fueled wave of uninhibited freedom.

The thrill of your first time is a great feeling to pursue at every age. Whether you're thirty, forty, fifty, or sixty, we all face moments in life when we need a new story. A reboot. A new idea of who we can possibly be.

I worked with Sara Arnell at the Arnell Group for seventeen years. I always say that anything I know about marketing and advertising, I learned from Sara. But maybe I should say "because of Sara," since I also learned so much from some of the uniquely talented people who were my partners at that agency.

When I was trying to sort through my post-Maybelline life, Sara said, "You should teach. At Parsons."

I had never taught. Immediate shift into turbo fear. "Don't college professors have to be really smart? You know, PHDs and dissertations and that stuff?"

Sara explained that Parsons loved "professional practitioners"—people working in the business who bring the real world to the classroom. In an instant, I knew that this was the do-something-that-scares-you opportunity I needed. For ten years now, I've taught one course each semester: PUDM 2315: Marketing, Public Relations and Branding.

When people hear that I teach at Parsons, they often ask, "Do you know Tim Gunn?" I do not know Tim, but he is the poster boy for creating a brilliant Act 2. "Just Tim It" should be the tagline for human reinvention.

Teaching scared me. Prepping the course syllabus was, in its own way, an audit of my career to date. It was daunting. What the hell did I know that was of any value to a twenty-year-old? What case studies in my portfolio might sound cool to a millennial? Was "cool" even the right word? How could you organize and communicate something you did instinctively and unconsciously?

Then I read what those kids paid to go to Parsons. I wasn't just scared; I was petrified. I needed to be sure my class delivered real, off-the-charts value. If I was going to be a "professor," I had to become a *professor*. I chased every resource that could prepare me for the first day of class. Over my ten years, I've audited classes online to see how colleagues teach their classes. I'm in constant conversation with my teaching cohort, picking up new content and fresh ideas about how and what to teach .

I have the luxury of only teaching one class each semester. Anyone who thinks they work hard because they have early breakfast meetings, client dinners, or business travel should shut up and do the happy dance. I've been one of you. That's a lucky life. Our army of educators never get served a little ramekin of warm nuts or a gooey cookie while they prep, teach, grade, and counsel a full roster of classes.

Fear can be the great immobilizer. Fear can be terrifying and overwhelming. Who isn't afraid of being poor, alone, or lost at sea (literally or metaphorically)? Fear can also be inspiring. It's good if it makes you productive. Fear made me overprepared for every meeting I ever entered.

Fearlessness is a gift from god. My friend Brian is like a slot machine of random but interesting facts. He blew my mind when he peppered our conversation with this mystifying tidbit: "Do you know 40 percent of people do not have an inner dialogue?"

"How is that even possible?" I'm incredulous, sounding like Maggie Smith.

"So, you're like me?"

"The squirrels in my head never sleep."

"Most of the day, I'm easily juggling three thoughts at once."

Later that night, I ask ChatGPT about this. I mean, it just seems impossible.

Chat: It's interesting to note that around 40 percent of people experience a lack of inner dialogue, which can vary significantly in how individuals process thoughts and emotions. This phenomenon raises questions about cognitive styles, self-reflection, and communication.

I prompt: Is there research?

Chat: Yes, there is research on the phenomenon of inner dialogue and its absence. Studies explore the cognitive, psychological, and neurological aspects of how people think, and significant findings have emerged about the variations in inner experiences among individuals, including its role in self-regulation, problem-solving, and emotional processing.

If your inner voice isn't much of talker, if you're in the 40 percent that are born fearless, then listen to the advice of friends—it could be what you need to hear and do. But if your brain is set on a permanent spin cycle, somewhere in there is the information you need to tackle your fears.

In reality, if the thing that scares you doesn't work—if it's a total bust—just remember, it's also a blip. Everything eventually winds up in the past. It's like with this book—if I even share it with anyone, if they roll their eyes behind my back, if agents or publishers say no, no one will ever know. But if one day, I'm taking a few questions at a book signing and someone asks, "What made you decide to write a book at your age?"

"I did it because it scared me. But in a good way."

"YOU SHOULD WRITE A BOOK!"

Research often highlights things we just don't see.

After my ridiculous stint trying to solve mascara emergencies for Maybelline, I was swimming in a soup of uncertainty. I conducted an informal and unscientific survey of friends and family: "If you were me, what would you do next?"

Five out of ten friends hit the same idea: "Become a real estate agent."

Real estate is dependent on the kindness of contacts and referrals. I agree with my friends: I know lots of people, and I meet lots of people. I'm organized and communicate in a precise and concise way.

Also, I would be a horrible real estate agent. If I spent my day showing homes twice as nice as mine, I'd be the snarkiest realtor in the Hamptons. We all know there are people who have more and less than we have. "More," I'm okay with. However, "holy-shit more" tilts my world. If I were showing a "holy-shit home" to a technillionaire, I'd hate them and me in equal measure. If you're a realtor, resentment doesn't help build business.

When I look at real estate porn online, I lose perspective. Like *Alice in Wonderland*, I am sucked into Sothebys.com—a world of wonder that's equally infuriating. I know many people would be very happy to move into my house, and I know that it's a real luxury to have both "town and country." However, I can't help but envy a water view or property with landscaped perfection. When I see a "premiere property," in my mind, I instantly start living in that house. In my dream life,

I wake up in a house that's part *Wallpaper Magazine* and part Nancy Meyers movie. Visually, it' unsettling and disturbing, but dreams are never linear. I dive deep into the fantasy. I conjure up a midsummer night's dinner party, cashmere Christmas gatherings, and winter game nights with creative charcuterie boards and brown-butter-infused bourbon concoctions. It is a carefully curated, perfectly art-directed vision of a life that's in another zip code and tax code.

My other challenge as a realtor? Facing the horror of other people's stuff. Their clutter. Their collectibles. The bad art. Evidence of a Home Goods addiction. The crazy accumulation of Crock-Pots, hair dryers, flea-market treasures, old jeans, run-to-death sneakers, hopeless cosmetics, gunky shampoo bottles, and creepy dolls. I may not be a realtor ,but one thing I know: If you are selling a house, put your dolls away. Or send them to camp.

So, the answer to suggestion number one is a definitive "No way!" I am not and never could be a realtor.

Then – and I paraphrase – four respondents deflect with a dismissive tone: "Don't ask me shit like that! I can't even figure it out for myself."

That brings us to suggestion number three (one response): "Write a book."

Realtor or writer? I never thought of myself as someone with such limited options.

I tend to wrestle my demons by talking about them. If I verbalize what's on my mind, the fog of confusion starts to lift. If I talk it out, it often helps me see past the blind spots. Luckily, I have a few friends who indulge these conversations, I assume because they're on a similar journey, or they're happily avoiding work.

I was twenty minutes into a bunch of blah, blah, blah with my friend Michelle:

"…and it's not just me. This quest for a second act at any age needs to be recognized and codified."

"Hmm." Michelle is either thinking or doing Wordle. Like Katie Couric, her questions push in a positive direction. "This search for Act 2—it's needs to be a thing, right?"

"Maybe I should do a naming exercise?"

Michelle half-heartedly suggests, "Maybe start with a hashtag? Like, #rewiring instead of #retiring. Is that a movement?"

"Definitely a too-cute T-shirt."

I can hear Michelle thinking.

When Michelle has an idea, she can sound like a judge handing down your sentence: "You should write a book."

Michelle is strategic. She's marketing-savvy. She's clear and emphatic. Coming from her, "You should write a book!" sounded like a declaration of fact. Michelle worked in the White House. Her advice carries the weight of a policy proposal. So, if you're reading this book and think, *What a bunch of horse shit!*, don't blame me. Blame my friend Michelle.

I didn't jump right into it, but Michelle's challenge never left me. It's always there, whispering in the wind, "You should write a book!" I leave in "whispering in the wind" as a reminder that writing a book requires critical edits and numerous rewrites. "Whispering in the wind" sounds like the title of an unreleased Joni Mitchell album.

Writing a book is definitely something that scares me, but for now, I'm focused on being able to hold a warrior pose when I'm out on my paddleboard.

TXT CHAIN: March 2020

Missed you in class.

I'm done for now.

Yoga is cheaper than therapy.

No. I'm done. This Covid shit is getting serious.

Really think so?

Know so. They shut down Broadway.

They did? Oh—I've got a bunch of tickets in April?

Well, the show ain't going on.

But it's like a month from now…

Get masks. Plastic gloves. Beans. Rice. Flour. Sugar. Fill your freezer.

You're scaring me.

Good. I hope you're stocked up on Purell and toilet paper.

No—I was in LA on business.

LA gets the news.

I was off the grid.

And that's a euphemism for what…?

You can fill in the blank.

Go now. Grocery store. Drugstore. Stock up. Cookie dough. You'll want cookies. And puzzles—go on Amazon and order puzzles.

Vodka, too, I guess.

Yes—vodka. Whatever they have. Even if it's Absolut.

Nobody saw it coming. Well, maybe a few people knew it would come one day, but no one knew that at the start of 2020, a global pandemic would force the world to rethink life and how we live it.

In many ways, for the time being, we couldn't be who we were:

- Social animals were forced to stay home.
- Culture vultures couldn't be "the first" to see the latest and greatest.
- Influencers' selfieness wilted in lockdown.
- Sports fans had no one to root for.
- The life of the party was reduced to a Zoom screen.
- Fashionistas were all dressed up with nowhere to go. Like that proverbial tree falling in the forest, fashion needs an audience.

No matter who you were or where you lived, you were forced to ask the questions, *Now what? Who am I if I can't see myself reflected in my work, my family, my friends?*

COVID-19 lumped us all into this same existential crisis, this extended intermission in the drama, comedy, and romance of our lives. We were living in the same uncertainty.

I don't journal. Never have. I don't take photos, even on vacation. I don't catalog my feelings with a therapist. But for some reason, I sent myself an email with this bit of randomness. I felt, for the first time in my life, that I was intensely focused on "right now." Rather than regretting the past or worrying about the future, I was locked up in the present:

YOUR PAST IS PAST IF YOU STOP RELIVING IT.
YOUR FUTURE WILL FOREVER BE UNCERTAIN.
WHAT YOU REALLY NEED TO KNOW IS WHERE YOU ARE RIGHT NOW.
YOU ARE THE STORY YOU'RE LIVING RIGHT NOW.

And then I probably, blithely, watched another episode of *Happy Valley* or *Killing Eve*.

"CAN I WRITE A BOOK?"

During my masked-up, gloved-hands stealth drives to grocery stores and essential errands, I spent a great deal of time interrogating this question.

Can I write a book?

I had never been proficient or efficient working through doubt.

At the time, I thought, *Writing a book would be a secret.*

Writing could prevent me from biting my fingernails, which intensified while absorbing the news of a world in lockdown.

My idle fingers reach for carbs in any form, so, for me, writing is also weight management.

I decided if, on some level, Michelle was interested in my BS, then maybe other people would be too. But it was an abstract idea. An intellectual ping. Easily ignored for now.

In marketing terms, the assignment is defined and detailed in a brief. Since time is money and creative time is very expensive, every initiative has a brief that is carefully crafted by the client and agency to ensure that all work is directed at the bulls-eye of success.

The brief is the North Star—the source of clarity and conviction.

The brief defines the end game.

It establishes the market, competition, and opportunity.

First question and first answer on the brief: What are we talking about? The brief for a new TV spot specifically asks for a thirty- or sixty-second spot. Sometimes twenty seconds, with a ten-second "tag."

Tags tell the customer where to buy it locally, like, "Available only at Target while supplies last," followed by all sorts of warnings, caveats, and legally mandated qualifiers.

I started writing a bunch of essays. Stuff. Smushy. Pointless. When I accepted my own challenge to shape it into a book, I needed a brief with a clearly defined deliverable. First question: *How many pages should this book be?*

Simply asking that question made me imagine the bitchiest reviews ever. How would I feel if my first review opened with, "At 271 pages, *The S@#t I've Heard at Yoga* is 271 pages too long." Flash—another critic's punny dismissal: "The shit he heard at yoga makes for a crappy book."

But it's a long way from starting a book to worrying about its critical reception.

I always do what every marketer does: I research. I hunt and gather information to create an informed context.

For this endeavor, I simply googled "word count." According to commonplacebook.com, Tolstoy jammed 527,287 words into *War and Peace*. Thank god I wasn't writing that book. Partnering with the "Tools" tab on Word, I saw that I was at 30,879 words, and I'd only been writing for four months.

I liked that pace. It was a pace I could sustain and still have time to do Wordle, Connections, and Strands. I could participate in all my text chains, a few of which required a competitive bit of wit.

John Irving's *A Prayer for Owen Meany* was a shocking 257,154 words. You see, what distinguishes Owen as a character and fuels his story is that he's very, very short. Perhaps that's why I remember the book being shorter than the word count indicates. I love John Irving. *Cider House Rules* ranks as one of my top five reading experiences. *Owen Meany* is my second favorite Irving book. Most people would argue that *The World According to Garp* is his best work, but it's only number four on my list. I think most people cite *Garp* because, truth be told, they've only seen the movie.

I kept searching for something that might provide a better bull's-eye. *Cold Mountain* was 161,511. With that book, I desperately wanted to read "The End" after 3,025 words. In spite of the tortuous crawl of that book, I forced myself to see the movie because the only way the Oscars are interesting is if you've seen all of the nominees. With *Cold Mountain*, every word of both the book and the movie left me *very* cold.

Harper Lee scrambled up a paltry 100,388 words into the beloved *To Kill a Mockingbird*. Something told me she spent a good deal of time working and reworking her text to get that much story into so few words. I didn't have to reach legendary status with the book I was writing. I don't have that ambition.

While I actively avoid being the center of attention, I did have a short list of people I'd love to run into and offer up an invite: "Oh—well, if you're in town, stop by my book party!"

That was the kind of answer I needed to the question, "What's new?"

The Devil Wears Prada was around 95,000 words, *Ironweed* was 67,606, *The Hours* was 54,243 words, and *The Bridges of Madison County* hovered around 50,000 words. All four books inspired really, really good movies that showcased the chameleon talents of Meryl Streep. These somewhat shorter books told the compelling stories of very complex women and earned Meryl four of her twenty Oscar nominations. Hmm, perhaps a good barometer of a book's success is whether or not it holds the promise of becoming a vehicle for Streep?

I could've continued my googling, but I really wanted to figure out my target word count before I walked the dog. *The Color Purple* was 66,556 and that book did very well, even finding success as a movie and a Broadway musical. If I maintained my same level of productivity for six months, allowing for respites, rewrites, and a few weekend guests, I was going to have 65,000 words by the year-end holidays. I could be finished with my (first?) book at the start of 2022. I liked that timing. Surely, Covid be would over by then.

I allowed myself a moment to imagine that maybe, I might "put it out there" and maybe it would get published. Was it this creative endeavor or the yoga that was generating newfound energy and a new sense of who I might be? Was I becoming more confident or just less fearful?

I settled on a goal of 45,000–55,000 words. That seemed like it would have a respectable heft for this type of book. I didn't want to be signing something that felt like a pamphlet, but I didn't want a book so cumbersome you wouldn't want to carry it with you on a plane. A lot of books get read on planes. I added that to the brief: *Keep it grab-and-go.* I'm sure that, just like my mom, your mother taught you, "Don't ever overstay your welcome." Hopefully, I wouldn't be overstaying my word count.

One more thing about John Irving. When I first moved to New York, my run typically looped me into Central Park. I'd sometimes see John Irving running, his humpy wrestler's body pounding forward on the dirt path around the reservoir. He was who I wanted to be: a unique talent and master storyteller. His clever writing always made my brain smile. In 2000, his script for *Cider House Rules* won him the Oscar for Best Adapted Screenplay. In truth, there's never been a movie version of his work that comes close to the exhilaration of reading his cleverly constructed and often heart-twisting prose. No—not even *Garp*! *Garp* is a movie that made people who don't read feel good. It was a literary quick-fix. Like many movies adapted from books, seeing *Garp* provided a shortcut to feeling like the old you who used to read.

Other than devouring his books and staring at his ass during my loop around the Central Park reservoir, I'm confident that John Irving and I have nothing in common. I can't imagine that on a cold winter evening he curls up in a cable knit sweater and sweatpants to see what hijinks befuddles the real housewives of Beverly Hills. But really, who knows? I was often surprised by who watched *Project Runway* (the early years). People—interesting people—are all a little high/low in everything they do.[1]

I know what you're thinking: *What's the point here?!*

Writing this chapter took me back to John Irving and the books I read when I had a thirty-two-inch waist. I was reminded of a version of me that's been packed away in storage bins in the back corners of my mind. It brought to life a dream only half-pursued and partially realized. Like yearbooks and old concert paraphernalia, it felt good to touch that uncensored energy of youth. That felt like how I used to be. That former me was a little more fearless. A little more assured in my aspirations. Driven by accomplishment rather than the trappings of success. I wanted to get together with that version of me again.

We should have lunch, my brain screamed inside my head.

Revisit who you were.

Remember who you wanted to be.

Find the ideas and aspirations you put away or put aside.

Maybe you're not going to pursue the same dream, but there's a part of the new you to be found in the younger, rough-draft versions of the younger you.

Caution:
There's value *and* danger in remembering who you didn't become.

**DON'T TRIP OVER
POSSIBILITIES OR REGRETS.**

This slide I share with start-ups.

Typically, start-ups try to do too much all at once.

---

[1] Ayn Rand watched *Charlie's Angels.* I put this in a footnote because she's controversial, and I don't want it to become a distraction. Most people skip the footnotes. Apparently, she was a big fan of Farrah Fawcett. In fact, she wanted Farrah to play Dagny Taggart in a film version of *Atlas Shrugged.* When Ayn passed away, they found a Farrah doll under her couch. Ayn Rand had a Farrah Fawcett doll! You may not like Ayn's politics, but you can't say this isn't an interesting footnote.

Fearless enthusiasm, amazing ideas, and boundless energy are the key capital of a startup and the essential ingredients of success. But they can quickly propel a small company into oblivion.

You can do too much all at once.

A clear objective provides a path for decision-making.

That means saying no more than saying yes to all those great ideas that fly around on Slack.

Like teenagers, start-ups make mistakes because they don't yet understand the value of boundaries.

Mistakes are our best teachers…if you move beyond your failures.

Like a startup, you can't spend time with any regrets about what didn't happen on the road to becoming you.

You have all the time you need for whatever you want to do *if* you wake up every day with a clear objective.

No, that's not marketing bullshit.

It sounds like it, but let's do the math.

Let's say people reading this book have twenty good years ahead of them.

That's a lot of time to live with an outdated version of yourself.

It's like hanging on to a Blackberry. Good luck trying to get an UBER with that.

Now imagine you are twenty again. At that age, there wasn't a day you didn't think to yourself, "By the time I'm thirty, I'm going to ____________" (fill in your blank). Those ten years that stretched out in front of you seemed like forever. It was an ocean of time. A decade was plenty of time to make your mark. With age, time seems to pass more quickly. Not true. Time is a constant. Ten years is ten years. Why is it, then, that you never hear a sixty-year-old say, "By the time I'm seventy, I'm going to win an Oscar." Why not? No matter what age you are, whether you're thirty, forty, fifty-five, or sixty-something, you still have enough time to set the world on fire. Or, at least, embrace the newfound energy that comes with trying.

Based on my early years as a writer, I knew I didn't want to reenlist for the cycle of rejection, hope, and uncertainty that engulf creative endeavors. But I also knew I was building a shaggy mess. So, I decided to write with purpose. I challenged myself to leave the safety of a playtime mindset.

Write like you mean it, I told myself. *For the hell of it.*

Old me rummages through the corners of my mind, hunting for squirrels that can sabotage my *yes* energy.

New me reminds me,

Lean to the light.

Don't break your own heart.

Allow more. Don't overachieve.

Don't think your way through this.

Just do do do.

Not too long ago, you had to have an educated relationship with a typewriter to even dabble in a little bit of prose. Today, everyone has a keyboard. Email has transformed all of us into decent typists. In email terms, writing a book is the equivalent of writing four way-too-long emails every day for six months. Sitting here, in this moment, having written thousands of emails, I can say, with unequivocable confidence, that writing a book is the bigger challenge. When writing a book, you can't rely on a pic of Sarah Sanders in an unfortunate, horizontally striped dress to get a laugh.

Like any marketer, I started imagining the product. The name. The package. I had no critical reputation or devoted following. I needed a catchy title. I needed a cover that indicates a humorous read—but not cute. Maybe something graphic. I wanted my hypothetical book to be serious fun—helpful but entertaining.

If you're writing a book, you have something to do all the time. When asked, "What's up?", you can always say, "I've been working on my book." That's a much better answer than "not much" or reporting out that Joy Reid changed her hair yet again.

Writing a book, even a bad book, requires fortitude and discipline. It's a brave act. A solo expedition to your North Pole. If you have a story to tell, then you've lived. If you have horrors to share, then you've survived. If you've been given the talent, drive, focus, and determination to write a book of complete fiction, then you know the value of waking up with purpose and passion. If you're writing science fiction, you've dared yourself to explore the big unknowns. If you are squeaking out your first novel between gigs at Sweetgreen and Trader Joe's, you are truly extraordinary.

I was not any of the above. I was a privileged person in Covid lockdown who, at that moment—along with the whole world—was facing an uncertain future. But I had plenty of cheese to get me through it. Cheese has always been my drug of choice.

In the Great Lockdown, I couldn't go to yoga. I embraced isolation.

Like Michelle said, I could write a book…just to stay sane.

It could be my pandemic project.

After all, there was nothing at stake. If I never finished my book, if it never found a publisher or failed to find an audience, if nothing else, I would have examined where I'd been, assessed where I was, and hopefully discovered where I wanted to go next. After Covid.

Sitting up straight in my chair, shoulders back, I assumed the posture of writer. Well, a writer who does yoga. Shoulders round to the back, away from the ears.

Breathe in to the count of eight.

I began.

Breathe out to the count of eight. Hold.

Breathe in….

Tap tap tap. Immediately, I was all in. Sequestered away in isolation, I had the escape I needed.

The working title was *Shirtless in a Snowstorm*, but that didn't sound like a fun read.

If you can't come up with the three to eight words that make a good title, maybe you shouldn't write a whole book.

Similar to yoga, with writing, you learn a lot every time you go to your mat.

"WHO NEEDS OR WANTS THIS BOOK?"

I add yoga apps to my Apple TV. I'm never in sync with the flow.

I try a Zoom class.

Whatever dreamlike escape I was hoping for evaporates.

Class ends. Virtual yoga makes me miss real life.

The squirrels come marching in.

A particularly bitchy squirrel lobs a deadly grenade: "Who is ever going to wanna read this book?"

I remind myself of something I heard or read at some point: "Doubt asks the questions that need answers. Doubt is the precursor of focus."

"You know," bitchy squirrel continues, "you've gotten so good at bullshit that you no longer know if the story in your head is genuine or just spin."

Bitch squirrel caught me.

"Who?" That's the question I tell my students they must always ask. "Who?"

Before you design a product, write an ad, or start building your brand, you have to ask, "Who?"

Who are you talking to?

Who are you selling to?

Who needs or wants what your peddling?

I wasn't handed a brief for this book.

I didn't do research about my potential consumer.

SFX: An impatient car horn.

Someone wants my parking space.

It's summer—panicked drivers in search of parking spaces stalk you as you walk to your car.

I've been sitting here talking to myself.

I don't remember a single moment of my yoga class. My brain has been held captive, wondering, *Who? Who is my who?*

I need a "who." Having a clear "who" will give shape and purpose to this dialogue I'm having with myself.

I'm looking for the people who can't get from here to there—from a bad place to a good place. From a bad job to a smart move. From suddenly being alone in the world to embracing change. From midlife crisis to fifty, or fifty to sixty, or sixty to destination unknown. From feeling powerless to feeling like you're in a Ram Truck Super Bowl spot. From standing shirtless in a snowstorm to lovin' life. I know there are many of me out there. I can see it in the eyes of people I know. It's that unsettling assertion of a false confidence. I see it in the tense smiles of new people I meet; they have that look that says, "I wish you were meeting the real me from ten years ago."

It's there on the faces of strangers in line to see a sadly mediocre Diane Keaton "I'm older but I still want to have sex" comedy. There's a lot of people like me who are certainly uncertain about where they are in life. They have that nagging thought, *Who am I if I'm not quite my old self?*

Who am I if I lose my airline status?

Who am I if I enter The View *into my DVR cue?*

Who am I if I have the time to overreact to the annoying redesign of Hulu's navigation?

Who am I if have no good reason to shave today?

There's comfort knowing you are not unique, but that's a salvo, not a solution. If you're a boomer, you've been around for a while. In our work, lives, and community, we had a role to play. Our value proposition was solid. We were doers, leaders, and parents. We were funny, responsible, supportive. We organized, socialized, and entertained. We traveled, exercised, cooked, and decorated. We won tennis matches and completed marathons. We accomplished, succeeded, moved up, and moved on. We invented, innovated, disrupted, and remade the world. We made pickleball happen. We mattered. At least that's how we saw ourselves. The "youngers" see us through a very different lens: capitalistic hedonists and climate whores.

For younger generations, the questions might be the inverse. If I never get close to my dreams, who will I become? If I don't have what I want, when should I stop going for it? If the future isn't a hopeful destination, then what's the point? If senior year was my best year yet, will I always be living in the past?

No matter what age you are, we all have pictures of who we used to be. There's you with your first love. There's a headshot from when you thought you wanted to be an actor. There's you, on your first day as a first-grade teacher. There's you with bangs. With a moustache. With a gondolier in Venice. There's you, the life of the party before your name changed to Dad. There are so many pictures from when you lived in New York or Chicago, ran a marathon, saw Bruce, Prince, Tina, Billy, Beyonce, or the Dead, joined the air force, studied dance, shared a ski house with college friends, worked at Facebook, spent two years in the Peace Corps, auditioned for *Project Runway*, or made out with a cowboy at your bachelorette party in Nashville. In those moments, you were where you were supposed to be. In those pictures, you looked like you.

Whether it's ten, twenty, or thirty years later, in moments when we don't know who exactly we are now—when life, love, or career is upended—the photos of our past selves can cause paper cuts in our heart.

Will I ever be that happy again?

Will I ever be confident, hopeful, or cool again?

Will I ever be that in love again?

If your routine is rudely interrupted by circumstance, free time can be uncomfortable.

The questions start.

Maybe I should move?

Maybe I should find a therapist? Am I the only one I know that doesn't see a shrink?

Maybe I should try yoga?

Maybe I'll take pottery classes or…?

The first three options deserve consideration. Obviously, I'd highly recommend option three. But option four? Big no! If you want pottery, go to Copenhagen. It's a great city. The food is quirky (that's where I ate baby pine cones), the coffee is good but overhyped, and, without even trying, you'll find amazing pottery.

The space in your head needs to be a no-parking zone. Adults, like children, need parental controls on their unstructured time. Encouraging a child's imagination is critical to their personal development. Imagination is the perpetual engine that redesigns our world. But a fully formed adult's imagination can spin into fester mode. As they say in the world of screenwriting, "Mischief ensues." Squirrels start clawing around in our heads, tearing away at confidence and self-esteem. As my friend JT said, "Before you know it, you're driving down Further Lane, headed to the beach, wondering what it would be like to just drive head-on into the ocean."

That's problematic, particularly if you have an expensive car fully loaded with electronic features. I'm not concerned that JT is seriously considering this bit of off-roading, but if that's a sample of his regular programming, he needs to get out of his head.

Dark clouds hover over everyone. If I think about me too much, I start playing nihilistic philosopher, asking myself, *How it is possible to stay happy for another twenty years?*

If you have twenty years.

And are you really all that happy?

I don't even fucking know what happy is….

If you're going down the rabbit hole to Regret-ville, if you're wondering where you might have taken a wrong turn, sign up for a six-month trial subscription to Sirius XM and listen to Howard Stern. What's inside Howard's head is much more interesting than your inner voice. Too much time alone in your head can leave you stuck in the fear-gear.

Podcasts, books on tape, YouTube—we are in the golden age of distraction. If you're in a winter of discontent, throw on some headphones and let other voices drown out your inner monologue.

I now see the genius of early bird specials! Old people can't wait another minute to get out of the house. They know that when they're home alone, they focus on their aches and pains. They get sucked into their fears. They're in the third act of their play. Time is ticking. They want to get to dinner as early as possible. They want to change the picture playing in their head.

You may not be headed to an early bird special, but if your life is in transition, you need a new picture of you. A picture of who you want to be right now. And five years from now.

Everyone winds up in an uncertain holding pattern at least once or twice in their life. That's a lot of people who might find value in this book.

I realize, in these past few chapters, I have become my own yogi—spitting out tidbits of emotional nutrition.

And so, my confidence returns.

I get out of my head and back to the page.

Fist pump—write on!

I take a minute to admire the tenacity of writers. There I am—instant recall: trying to carve out a career as a writer, waiting for agents to call, endless introspection. A tiny check arrives. I can feel the sun again. Short-lived lifelines of acceptance but mostly drowning in waves of rejection.

Let's level set with a few hard facts:

According to NPD BookScan—which tracks about 85 percent of bookstore, online, and other retail US print sales of books (including Amazon.com)—only 789 million print books were sold in 2022 in the US in all publishing categories combined, both fiction and nonfiction (*Publishers Weekly*, January 9, 2023).

That's not even three hundred copies per book in the U.S. No writer is buying a Birkin bag with those sales. Okay, even if you add in ancillary sales (e-book, audio, and foreign sales), most books don't even sell a thousand copies over their lifetime.

Granted, the figures are skewed because of the tsunami of self-published books which mostly depend on the kindness of friends and family to generate their miniscule sales figures.

But traditionally published books aren't paying off mortgages or buying boats either. A BookScan study of print retail sales in the US by the top ten publishers found that only 6.7 percent of the new titles released by these companies sold more than ten thousand copies in their first year of sales, only 12.3 percent sold more than five thousand copies in their first year, and only 33.9 percent sold more than one thousand copies in their first year.[2]

"Yeah—but then there's Grisham, Rowling, Ann Rice…"

John Grisham only sold five thousand copies of his first book, *A Time to Kill.* But that didn't stop him. And that's my point: There is a tenacity at work that's mysterious and just crazy. I'm sitting here playing this game of sentence structure and wordplay because I have the time. This is not a gold rush. The bestseller list is not routinely minting new millionaires. Writers are like intellectual gladiators; they step into the ring, knowing full well they'll be going home broke. There are millions of books published each year. We certainly don't need more writers. We need more readers.

---

2 Kristen McLean's response to the blog "No, Most Books Don't Sell Only a Dozen Copies" by Lincoln Michel, September 4, 2022.

"THINK ABOUT WHAT YOU CAN DO, NOT WHAT YOU CAN'T DO."

When I first heard this, I immediately thought:

Lame. Feels a little bit like "everybody gets a medal."

That was a few years ago, early in my practice.

Today, I wake up in a heavy blanket of dread. I hate my banana. Too soft. Bad start to the day but it's not the banana's fault. It's the damn book. If I stop, I'm a failure. If I continue, I have to be honest about my limitations.

I'm learning—the hard part of writing a book is writing the book.

This morning, I have more reasons to stop than reasons to keep going.

Last night, I was overflowing with confidence and determination. I imagined my book tour, snuggling up on Amtrak as I make my way around the charming towns of New England. I'd sign books in the evening and wake up to fresh-baked scones in idyllic cozy inns. My "literary" tour would look very much like a Vermont tourism calendar. I'd check into rooms that might be featured in a Taschen pictorial album of fantasy cabins. I'd read from my book—this book—outfitted from the pages of a Todd Snyder catalog.

I get carried away from reality very quickly. My imaginary book tour has a much better chance of becoming reality if I finish the book. Unfortunately, yesterday's "I got this" bravura gives way to today's "WTF—nobody will be at my book signings because nobody is going to buy my book. Even if I find an agent who lands a publisher, no one browsing the new releases at BookHampton is going to reach for *The S@#t I've Heard at Yoga* instead of a new book from Amor Towles or Zadie Smith."

Think about what you can do, not what you can't do.

Okay.

"Yes! I can finish this book."

Even if no one ever reads it, just sitting here talking to you, my imaginary reader, is giving my day purpose. If I wasn't doing this—if I surrendered to the tyranny of my doubts—I'd be swimming in a cesspool of regret. I'd be reviewing everything I've never accomplished in life, such as never winning that Oscar for my first screenplay, never going to Egypt, and never learning to ice skate. Of course, once I start down that rabbit hole, there are many lingering questions with the power to help me hate myself just a little:

Don't you wish you stuck with tennis?

Don't you wish you stuck with the piano? Or the guitar?

Don't you wish you had opted for braces back in high school?

Doubt is not a sustainable energy—it's a parking boot on the tire of your life.

Eliminate can't. Can you do that, Michael?

"Not sure—"

Can you try?

"I'll try."

"OMG! WHAT EXACTLY IS THE POINT OF ALL THIS?"

I hear you.

The point is: Listen to the advice you give others. You might just be talking to yourself.

I always advised people who were swimming in confusion to "write it down," to "get it out." Writing can help you organize your thoughts, freeing them from distracting emotion. Writing requires you to get to the facts.

I'm not saying you have to write a book.

Writing this book makes sense for me. Writing has been the cornerstone of my career, but, oddly, it's never been the core of my identity. Perhaps that's why I never achieved any significant impact as a writer. Hmm. See, committing your thoughts to paper can reveal hard truths.

Here's a key thing I learned at yoga: Not everything has to have a point. Some things just are. I recall an embarrassing class of stumbles and fumbles. I cornered my teacher.

"My poses sucked today. I couldn't hold a simple tree pose."

"Sometimes you just have an off day."

"Yeah—but why?"

"Not everything needs analysis. Not everything has an answer or a point. Somethings just are."

"Seriously?"

"More than seriously. You don't have to grade everything. It can just be."

"I don't know how to 'just be.'"

"Follow the detours. You don't always have to know where you're going to get somewhere good." She looks me in the eye, leaving me with a live-with-that nod.

Without even a glance back in my direction, she lobs a final thought: "Finding the point carries you forward."

Sitting at a red light, my phone beckons.

Yogi texts, "You never know what's down a road until you get there."

"WE SHOULD GET TOGETHER...."

The Covid vaccine gives us permission to put our toe back in the water of real life.

Being out and about, it feels like the world got beat up a bit.

But it's reassuring to know I can still buy monogrammed cocktail napkins, truffle cheese, and floral-scented tea candles.

Masked up, I return to the yoga studio.

Classes aren't full. People remain cautious.

Conversations are stilted; we're unsure of what may have happened to people or their loved ones.

Class begins. I'm emotional. I didn't know how much I missed this.

Usually, there's a lot of hugging in a yoga studio. Class ends. People maintain a respectful distance, but there's a noticeable and painful desire for human connection.

"Maybe we should get together?" is a suggestion I wasn't anticipating.

No.

No, maybe we shouldn't. And that has nothing to do with postpandemic fear.

Work. The gym. School. Yoga. They are all great places to meet people, but if you take that next step, whether it's a coffee, lunch, or god forbid, dinner—if it doesn't bloom into full friendship, then there's always residual weirdness every time you cross paths. You have to hyperpretend that you're happy to see each other even though it feels icky.

When someone says, "We should get together," be open, but proceed with caution. Just because you both enjoy a robust round of sun salutations, you never know who people are until they put on real clothes.

I've met some very good friends at yoga.

Yoga has made me more open to possibilities.

But yoga also teaches you to harness and maximize your energy.

There's little need to do more than what's required.

With practice, I've become more precise and selective in all of my choices. So when someone says, "We should get together," I quietly ask myself, *Should we?*

Most of my adult years, I was in the business of collecting friends. If I died suddenly, I wanted to go out confident that my funeral would be SRO.

I no longer expect to be friends with everybody.

Now, when I say yes to anything, I'm 100 percent committed to the person, the lunch, the night, the possibility.

On another day, it's damp and rainy. I'm piling on layers of clothes after class. I feign interest as a guy of like age recounts his career in advertising, searching for where we might have overlapped. Then there it is:

"We should get together...."

Before I can even begin to shape an ambiguous deflection, I get this: "You're not a sharer, are you?"

That's the end of my postclass bliss. Suddenly, I'm being assessed and analyzed—admittedly, with some accuracy.

Some people jump on the fast track to intimacy. They show you their scars and then they want to know where you hurt. They're scab pickers. Emotional vampires. They're bored with their own pain and want to smell yours. With me, they get impatient.

"You're not a sharer, are you?"

"I share. But maybe it's not what you're looking for?"

I've never been inclined to sit down at lunch and play show-and-tell with all my drama. I don't vomit my emotions into the lap of a new acquaintance. In New York, people just get right to it. When you meet for lunch, they don't want your history; they want your dirt.

My mind races back to a lunch almost thirty years ago.

"People don't move to New York to be boring. You've been here too long. You've got to have some shit. Come on—shock me."

"Even if I had secrets, I'd keep them secret."

"I know you have a dark side."

"Seriously, there's no kink. Nothing nasty. There's no story. It's just me and all my ordinariness."

"Then why do you whisper like everything is a big secret?"

"I long for a quieter world."

Admittedly, I play things close to the vest, like I'm ex-secret service. I don't like loud talkers. Growing up with a tyrannical father, crazy nuns, and a culture where even Liberace wasn't acknowledged as gay, whispering was an essential tool for survival. Whispering became my preset volume.

I am private.

I have no social media presence, mostly because I see it as a time suck.

I am protective of my time. I'm hyperconscious of time. I always have been. In fact, my mother took six-year-old me to a doctor because of my obsession with time. I was always in a panic that we'd be late for church or school or a movie. My Timex was my security blanket.

In addition to social platforms being the thief of truth and time, they feel like more of a "show" than an honest "share." Friendship for me is a contact sport; I want to see the whites of your eyes.

With this book, I have to change. "Write what you know" is standard advice given to all forms of writers. Translation: Dig deep into your personal story and spill the beans.

Step back.

Review what you've written.

Revise.

Reveal.

Morph into an open book. You have to know me on some level to be interested in what I have to share. You don't need my bio—that you'll find at the back of the book. If I have any chance of connecting with you through what I've learned at yoga, if you're going to trust what I've shared, you need some idea of what brought me to my "here and now."

So, here you go, an honest reveal. A genuine share….

"SHIRTLESS IN A SNOWSTORM (and the dawn of my ennui)."

I've never told this to anyone before.

Not even my husband.

I stood shirtless in a snowstorm.

On purpose.

And I loved it.

I was sixty-four and thinking about age more than I usually do. If you grew up with the Beatles, the song "When I'm Sixty-Four" is a dreaded omen lodged in your brain. Here I was, at that decrepit age Paul McCartney imagined when he wrote the song as a fourteen-year-old lad in England.

I was sober. Not even half of a gummy bear diluting my judgment. I'd only had two sips of a glistening, straight-up martini just prior to drifting out into the falling snow.

It was that first winter of COVID-19. With the post-Thanksgiving spike raging all around us, we remained steadfast in our isolation. Oddly, my husband, Randall, was in the city, probably visiting Dr. Toback, our eternally youthful dermatologist. We're both paying for the many years we insisted that a deep, dark tan was an essential accessory. With the removal of skin tags and basal-cell carcinomas, I probably have face time with Dr. Toback more often than I see some of my best friends.

I was home alone in East Hampton. We have a nice life, but we're not "beach rich." It's a seven-minute drive to the beach, unless we go to a bay beach. But bay beaches aren't real beaches. No screenwriter ever opened a script with:

EXT. BAY BEACH – SUMMER MORNING

If there's a beach in a movie, it's the real deal. Sand and surf glistening in sunlight or grabbing the light of the moon. No one falls in love on a bay beach.

The winter holidays were over. There were no vacations on the calendar. The future was blank. I was facing a disturbing void. It was a black night, begging for just a slim slice of moonlight. The back of our house is a wall of windows, so the darkness was enormous. The black space outside was much bigger and more ominous than the contentment I felt giving my martini a ten-count shake. Looking out into this abyss, you might expect that I'd have been paralyzed by a foreboding, horror-movie/boogie-man scenario. However, oddly, winter's dark night had a seductive, hypnotic hold over me.

Rewind to thirty minutes earlier.

I'm not sure how I wound up googling favorite movie scenes and Oscar highlights, but that's how I was wasting time that night. I've diagnosed myself as biproductive: I'm either hyperfocused and impressively prolific, or I start paddling on my keyboard into the Sea of Mindlessness. That night, the search algorithm somehow took me to a video of Johnny Mathis and Jane Olivor singing "The Last Time I Felt Like This" at the 1979 Oscars. Their duet from *Same Time, Next Year* was a nominee for best song.

Jane Olivor! My mind careened backward. I bet less than 0.5 percent of the people reading this book have ever heard of Jane Olivor. She was one of those tortured singers who specialized in wrist-cutting ballads. She sold out Boston concert venues, drawing hordes of drama queens and corduroy lesbians to her shows. Jane's audience came to her concerts as if being summoned by the Rapture. She had a haunting voice, and she knew how to edge a song. For Jane, every lyric was deeply personal, but for her audience, she was singing their story loud and clear. She sang with a longing that was both primal and impossible. Her music wasn't pop, dance, or easy-listening. Crossover appeal was always an unlikely event. Melissa Manchester figured out how to commercialize a bleeding heart into a sequined career, but Jane's painful lamentations never had the soaring, victorious crescendos that carried Melissa's defiant ballads to the top of the charts. Jane never took you to happy place. She was the Debbie Downer of divas. But she sure as hell was born to sing.

Jane Olivor was real and raw. She sang the truth, the whole truth, and nothing but the truth. There were no backup singers. And there definitely weren't any backup dancers. I was in my early twenties when I heard a Jane Olivor LP playing across the hall from my Cleveland Circle apartment, and, in that moment, I grew up just a little bit. My Woody-Allen "Manhattan" image of postcollege life was suddenly tinged with a few mean streets.

Looking back, the woman playing Jane Olivor across the hall was probably bipolar. Her large features carried too much makeup. Anytime I saw her coming or going, she looked like she just woke up from a nightmare. But she knew the words to every song on that album. Jane Olivor was Taylor Swift to the manic-depressives.

This is turning into a very long digression, and I don't want my personal brand to be "rambler." Where was I? Right—shirtless in a snowstorm.

Forty years later, sitting at my kitchen counter, I was held captive by a YouTube video. It propelled me into my very own Madonna "Ray of Light" kaleidoscopic memory trip, traveling through a stream of firsts back to my twenties and thirties. There was me—moving to New York. There was me the next night—moving through the crowd outside Studio 54. Yep, there I was, taking my place in the world of Calvin, Andy, Liza, and Patti Hansen—my favorite supermodel of all time. Snorting that first line of cocaine…hmm…not my thing. Thank god. Discovering poppers…way too much my thing. And there was me, hurt and confused the first time I was treated like a one-night stand. That very long day of dejected sadness—my very own Jane Olivor moment.

Then there I was, a little wiser, treating someone else like a one-night stand for the first time. There was me thinking, *Oh, now I get it*, and feeling so fucking grown-up. OMG—there I was, at the Film Centre Café with a young and thin Steve Bannon. Steve wanted to produce a play I'd written. Yes—*that* Steve Bannon. How crazy is that? You think, "I don't buy it," because I described him as thin. Steve was US Navy. And we were all a thirty-two-inch waist at some point. But the story of Steve is not going in this book. I like that a handful of dinners and meetings with young Steve Bannon give my personal brand a dash of "WTF?" peppered with a curious unpredictability.

For instance, my friend Meredith throws a dinner party at the start of every summer. Even if Meredith is just grilling hot dogs, her table is always set for a state dinner. Like her closet, Meredith's table has a lot of things that sparkle. One time, there was a gathering of about nine adults and one baby. The conversation twisted around the Parrish Art Museum and gay adoption and then took an odd turn into a debate about spray tans, which could only have been prompted by the mention of "never-going-to-win" candidate Donald Trump. Suddenly, Meredith lobbed the surefire conversation shifter, "Michael knows, well, knew, Steve Bannon." Needless to say, for at least four minutes, the floor was mine. People wondered how I knew him and what did I know. You're not reading this book for gossip; the title promised you'd be fed some sort of wisdom rooted in the practice of yoga. But if you ever attend a book signing of mine and you're dying to know more, you can ask me about Steve.

Back to my "Ray of Light" kaleidoscope. More firsts…moving to Los Angeles. I'm thirty-four and even the forty-four-year-olds look younger than me. A random chat with Joey from *Friends* at someone's birthday barbecue. Was it *his* birthday? My first break, a contract to write television pilots for Disney. The shocking realization that Tinker Bell could be a nasty little bitch. Seeing Madonna in concert. Seeing Madonna in a restaurant. Seeing a friend of a friend "romantically" linked to Madonna on *Page Six*.

I was surfing the memories and riding a rush of ecstatic energy. Randomness at the speed of light: Sitting on a speaker talking with Flea from Red Hot Chili Peppers at the premier party for *Singles*. Paul Reiser calling me at home to chat about *Mad About You.* Driving onto the lot at Sony to meet with him. Exchanging smiles with Helen Hunt. A friend winning an Emmy. Another friend getting an Oscar nomination.

And then *boom*! Like a clap of lightning, a realization creeps in: That feeling—that unbridled optimism, that dose of a nonchemically induced ecstasy—was the provenance of youth. It was the energy of "firsts"—that feeling like your story is still being written.

Sadness tiptoed up behind me. At some point, the montage of "firsts" forfeited the stage to memories of "loss." That phone call: "Your movie—they put it into turnaround." Suddenly, I smelled like old fish, the phone never rang, and big dreams morphed into pipe dreams. *Say goodbye to Hollywood.*

With every decision that's taken in life, a possibility is deflated. Friends move. Friendships disappear.

A very real sense of loss overwhelmed me. Jane Olivor was the perfect soundtrack for that winter night as I stared into the abyss. I was in love with the past, and it was never coming back. Sure, Paulina Porizkova was at my fortieth birthday dinner, and that was fun, but it was long ago. I remember it, but I am certain she doesn't. Looking back, I figure I've probably never made a permanent imprint on anyone's memory.

I slumped back in my stool, pulling away from the computer. I turned around and faced the darkness outside. As my eyes adjusted, gray details began to puncture the dark. Something glistened. Snow. I didn't remember the CBS weather guy telling me to expect snow. I moved closer to the glass; there was lots of snow. Beautiful, as always. Soft. Calming. Snow is like a drug. It can be enchanting. Dramatic. Quiet. Exciting. When you're twenty-three, you can't deny the exhilaration that comes with snow. Snow is fucking fun. And snow always made me want to get naked under the covers and tangle with another warm body. But now, at sixty-four, after a brief embrace of that youthful sense of joy, I remember that if the snow accumulates to more than six inches, I have to pay someone to shovel the flat roof of our modern home. At sixty-four, the poetry of snow melts away fast. I can hear Don Henley warning me that my days of innocence are over. My breath holds itself. I'm well on my way to becoming a jaded old fuck.

I don't have the best memory and certainly can't recall your name two minutes after meeting you, but I always remember what I was wearing when we met. On that snow-kissed night in the Hamptons, I was feeling cozy in black-and-white-checked flannel pajama bottoms and a gray cashmere turtleneck. The snow fell like glitter, seducing me into a dream. I slipped the sweater over my head. I opened the sliding door. With a racing heart, I moved outside, walking through a carpet of snow. Who hasn't wished they could live inside a snow globe? This felt exactly like that. Contained enchantment. Quiet. Perfect. Ideal. I stopped. I studied the barren oaks up-lit by the light pouring from the house. I'd never thought oaks were particularly pretty trees. Too thin. They don't carry a story, not like a giant elm. But that night, I saw the oaks for what they were. The oaks didn't care what I thought. They stood tall, never hoping to be shaped into anybody's landscaping schematic. Oaks expect to be marked for clearance; they know humans prefer grass. But the oaks remained that night, miraculously fighting off the forces of nature and second-home buyers.

I stood there in the miraculous quiet, snow sticking to my hair but melting against my skin. I had no sense of the cold. The snow didn't feel wet as it landed on my face and torso; it felt like a hundred kisses. As we do in yoga, I embraced a measured and purposeful inhale. This cold breath slowly filled my entire body. It fed my soul. Like all of us in our youth, common sense was often and brilliantly ignored, and in those moments of doing and dare, we discovered the truer and newer version of ourselves. Like Jane Olivor and Johnny Mathis, I couldn't remember the last time I felt like that…but I needed to feel like that again. I could not, would not, allow age and experience to blunt the tingling energy of standing shirtless in a snowstorm.

That was the moment my thoughts shifted into forward motion. I liked the extreme feeling of the cold; it was the polar opposite of comfy-cozy. The ironies of life were sitting in front of me: *How could I live my entire life and suddenly not know who I was?* I was never consumed by fear when I was young and broke, and I had been really broke around the age of forty. My total assets at that time were a Warhol cow print and a $28,000 credit-card bill. But I had a screenplay that just might sell. *Life is going to get good,* I thought back then.

Sure—I turned it around. New career. Money in the bank. Adult acquisitions that signal success on some level. So what was I worried about now? I didn't want to be the person who looked at snow and immediately thought about slush. I wanted snow to always and forever put me in a state of wonder.

Why do we forfeit the "why not?" gusto of youth to the young?

And so, it began. My search for the fountain of youth. Not to become ageless but to become as optimistic as my twenty-year-old self. To recapture the vitality of my thirties. The confidence of my forties.

So there I was, as many of you might be (metaphorically), shirtless in a snowstorm, the cold suddenly starting to sting, asking the universe, "Now what?"

"I WANT TO BE ANDY-HAPPY."

It's officially summer. There are people in class I've never seen before. It's probably my last Saturday class until fall—the crowds are back, and I'm not a fan of mat-to-mat classes. I'm drenched; humidity is back too. I'm gathering my stuff and actively resenting people who don't sweat. There's a young guy who, at first glance, could be Darren Criss, but he's just a gay guy from Los Angeles on the prowl for Instagram content—probably #namastehamptons. He's with a young woman who seems perfectly happy being his photo assistant. After a panicky spin to his better side, he thrusts himself into a gentle warrior pose. "We went to some cocktail, fundraiser, benefit thing. It was great. You don't see older gays in LA."

"Really?"

"Well, at a certain age, they go hide in Palm Springs."

"They must have been all over you."

"It was weird—they weren't. They're a different breed out here. I did get a side glance from Andy Cohen."

"Did you get a pic with him? #bravohamptons!"

"That's tricky energy. But he looked like honey bear don't give a shit."

"About what?"

"About anything. Looked like he couldn't care less. Might have been wearing J. Crew sales rack. He was chatting. Laughing. Like there was nothing famous about him. He looked like the happiest gay there."

"Well—he should be." Typing into her phone, she's clearly on the hunt for critical info. "He's building beachfront in Amagansett. Celebrity net worth says—"

"No. My ex had Andy kind of money, and he was a miserable fuck. It's not a money thing. Andy seems happy in a way most people don't. And if you listen to him on the radio—same thing—just fun, fun, fun. *That's* what I want!"

"What? Want what?"

"I want to be Andy-happy."

For those of you who maintain a low dosage of pop culture, Andy is his own kind of genius—the P.T. Barnum of wannabe celebrities. Most people who know Andy know him from his master creation, *The Real Housewives* franchise. The robust expansion of the *Housewives* lineup serves up a mindless metaphor for our times. We are living in Rome just before its fall. Bravo is the Colosseum where swords are replaced by snark. Andy provides the gladiators in the form of fake "housewives" with fake dramas. Fights ensue, but only after everyone's been to hair and makeup. It's more pageant than parable. Some may be repulsed by what they see as a tragic waste of time, but there's also a wildly enthusiastic audience. I'm sure the Romans were similarly split on the humanity of watching men and lions maul each other to the death. The Bravo housewives don't draw blood, but the claws are out, and the audience tunes in for the fights.

Andy has singlehandedly reinvented the soap opera with "unscripted" personal drama. He's built himself a big, rich life giving the people what they didn't even know they wanted. He's concocted his own formula for completely addictive entertainment. *Real Housewives* shows are the opioids of pop culture. Like any good recreational drug, they serve as the gateway to other Andy product. He is a multiplatform purveyor of glammed-up ordinariness, serving up TV, radio, books, and live appearances. Even when he's talking with a real celebrity on *Watch What Happens Live*—his dime-store, what-the-heck, late-night talk show—Charlize Theron or Jennifer Lawrence often wind up talking about the hate-to-love-'em housewives. He has cultivated a rabid fan base that is completely obsessed with his harem of overly eyelashed, turbo-glammed women.

I don't watch the housewives, but by osmosis, I can talk about them with some authority. That's scary. Very scary. It's like football—even if you don't pay any attention to sports, you somehow know who's in the Super Bowl.

"I want to be Andy-happy."

That kept playing in my head. What can that mean? Does Andy Cohen preside over a mythical fountain of happiness?

I start a deep dive. Going back and forth to yoga, I dial into Radio Andy on the Sirius channel. It's an all-talk channel that Andy programs with a Mardi Gras-roster of diverse talent. Every program on Radio Andy is a closed loop that circles around everything Andy—like a conversation painted by Escher. There's only a few hours a week that Andy is live on air, of course, mostly chatting about Andyworld.

It didn't take long before I shifted from anthropologist to happy listener. For the most part, Andy is a happy spirit. He's a welcome escape from the insanity coming out of the Trumpire.

In the car, I don't want to be challenged or alarmed. Car time is like plane time for me—a guilt-free plunder into medium-brow escapism, like watching Melissa McCarthy comedies or fashion documentaries.

Radio Andy is candy to my ears.

I'm at East Hampton Grill. For some reason, people are scanning their menus, which makes no sense to me. I know what I'm having because the menu never changes. Even the special is always the same. Or so it seems. There's me, thinking I've got *the* funniest story to tell: "I'm sitting in the car outside my own house, ignoring a desperate need to pee, listening to Andy spend way too much time fussing about his corduroy pants. I also bought a pair of wide-wale corduroys a few years ago that I never wear. It's impossible to make wide-wale anything work...."

I'm stabbed by a raised eyebrow from across the table. I realize I'm drowning in a you-had-to-be-there moment.

"I thought you'd be an NPR person."

"NPR always sounds like a damp and cold upstate dinner party. It's like getting into a long discussion about the proper use of the exclamation point. It's useful, but really?!"

A verbal spanking: "I'll text you a list of podcasts." I felt like Emily trying to absorb the dismissive stare down from Miranda Priestly in *The Devil Wears Prada.*

Ouch. A new squirrel has just been planted in my brain. In certain circles, Andy is like a bag of potato chips you hide until you're tucked away alone in your own home.

I don't know Andy. I've seen him three times in passing, but we've never spoken. I will say he is very smiley and acts taller than he is.

As a brand of entertainment, Andy's ability, talent, compulsion (all of the above) to share absolutely everything is fantastic. Andy talks about Andy's world all day long. That's his product. In real life, that gets tiring because most people are never as interesting as they assume they must be. You probably just thought, *And neither are you.* Andy has perfected the Art of Me—a talent and skill that's much harder than it looks.

Many people would stop me right here and say, "Warhol is the one who made 'Me' an art form!" Like Warhol, pop culture is Andy C's oxygen. In genius fashion, both Andys (or would it be Andies?) use pop culture to create more pop culture. I guess that makes Andy C. the king of meta-tainment. Warhol was famous but remote. He watched. He didn't really share. Andy is friends with *everybody*; he has friends in high and low places. It's a magical life overflowing with fabulousness. Andy's audience *loves* feeling like they're part of Andy's universe. He is your access to a party you'd never be invited to.

Others would make the case that Madonna or Kim K. are the masters of "Me." Madonna and Kim have armies of fans who draw inspiration from them even if they both seem a bit tortured by their own creations. There is strategy in every move they make. Madonna's stunning stream of reinvention feels informed by a focus group on "What's naughty now?" There's never been room for whimsy in her perfection.

She calculates what she wants our reaction to be. Madonna certainly doesn't owe us any more than she's given us. She promises bad-girl theatrics, and she delivers. But she's never really "in the room." She's in perpetual performance mode.

I don't know how much there is to know about Kim Kardashian, but she never ever seems to be having fun while making her millions. Even in her reality (or unreality) show, it's always a staged presentation of the real Kim. She may have been the first NFT, and we didn't know it.

Andy, on the other hand, runs on spontaneous energy. There's more joy and less calculation. His world is "loose." Less analyzed or thoughtful. Andy *is* what happens live.

Andy Cohen was born to be Andy Cohen, the greatest chitchatterer who ever lived. Colbert. John Oliver. Jimmy Kimmel—they're all good with the chitchat. Cable news is jammed with people who can talk all day long. But most on-air talent lives in the world of writing staffs, scripts, and teleprompters. Could they exist in an extemporaneous forum? If you take away the news, they may sit silent. If you were Gilligan-ed on a deserted island, there'd be no dearth of conversation if Andy had also booked that ill-fated three-hour cruise.

Listening to Andy stops the squirrels from taking over my brain.

We all have different questions that seem to play on a loop inside our head. They are the troubling, annoying, itchy questions that keep you company when you're alone. They're with you while you brush your teeth, trudge through an airport, or stand in line at Whole Foods.

If you run from these questions, you're running in the wrong direction. They are questions that have no answers. They are just there, always and forever. Things you'll never know, like, *Why you didn't I get that job? It was perfect for me!*

Why didn't I tell [name of friend] what I really thought. Why do I let them win every argument?

When's my big break coming? Or did it already happen and it was smaller than I was expecting?

Why didn't that thing with [insert name here] work out? It just ended before it ever really happened.

Am I retired? Or simply working differently? (As a rebrander might say.)

What the hell am I doing with my time? And not just today. Every day. It's not just "How do I fill up an afternoon?" It's more, "How do I fill up the rest of my life?"

This question is not unique to boomers. It's a challenge that can haunt you at any age—the torment that comes with wondering if you've missed the life you were supposed to live. You can be thirty-two, forty-one, or fifty-three and wonder, *Is this what the rest of my life is going to be?*

Drive time is open season for life's regrets to annihilate your peace of mind. There are many days when the sky is Disney blue but there's a nasty storm brewing inside my head. Right now, my question and quest is to find the key to being Andy-happy.

My presentations to clients always had a page of brand mandates; these were updates they needed to implement and opportunities they should embrace to maintain their edge in the market. Mandates highlight the strategic and creative guardrails for the work that lies ahead.

In Andy's world, people get to be their unedited selves. Andy invites everyone to rebel against themselves. He frees them from the strictures of expectations. The more comfortable people are when they're with you, the more they like you.

Noted.

Andy's success is not linked to a talent; it's the result of just being himself. Brash. Unapologetic. Joyous. Time with Andy never feels edited, calculated, or prepackaged. In our filtered, branded, scripted world, there's something brave about being your silly self.

Noted.

In Andy's world, there's always something new. And that's why people never tire of him. Andy's news is not always huge news, but he can transform the mundane into wish-I-was-there moments. He can make a night of karaoke sound more fun than a barrel of housewives. If you love what you're doing, that energy is always energizing.

Noted.

And then there's key marketing and branding questions: What is the essence of Andy? In everything he does, what is at the core of the Andy experience? What does he always bring to the table?

What did that LA insta-boy at yoga see in Andy that was unique?

What do I experience when I tune in Radio Andy?

With a little bit of thought, the answer becomes clear.

I had the same essence as Andy once, but I left it somewhere. Like my wedding ring, I didn't know I lost it until I realized it was gone.

What Andy exudes—and what I lack—is exuberance.

Andy is an energy force. Andy is a ball of exuberant, silly, unedited enthusiasm for just about anything that keeps people talking. He's not a critic or critical. He leans on observation rather than the weight of an opinion—a great strategy for someone in the business of being everybody's friend. It's not a bad strategy for life. You may not be known for what you think, but perhaps more people will think you're fun to be around.

I want to thank that young, gayfluencer who was in the Hamptons and working his better side to strike a happy pose. Andy-happy is the next pose I want to master.

DRIVE TIME

The shit I've heard in the car.

(If I hadn't taken up yoga, I wouldn't have heard any of this.)

"CUTE BRAS FOR WOMEN OVER FIFTY?"

Why does this keep happenin'? AI is not as smart as it wants to be.

I just did a surfer yoga class. It's like CrossFit meets yoga. There's not a single child's pose in the whole damn hour. The resting pose is a plank. Like hot yoga, I can only love this class when it's over.

I start the car.

Eleven texts. There's a lot of commentary about Kellyanne Conway today. A friend was seated across the aisle from her on a flight to West Palm Beach. They snapped a pic of her shoving a chocolate-covered pretzel into her mouth at 9:00 a.m. As we already knew, her mouth opens really wide.

Then I say good morning to my emails.

There is a definitive sense of dread and excitement.

There's that dependable mix of bad news and bad emails.

The Democrats always say good morning with end-of-the-world messaging in their subject lines.

Also begging for my affection are the digital ads for products that a smarty-pants algorithm determined are just what I need.

Sometimes they get it right.

I love the hatchet I bought from Best Made Co. It's a beautiful hatchet for which I have no use. I love having it for whenever I have something that needs chopping, which is never.

Now and then, Todd Snyder hits me with an Italian knit shirt I can't buy fast enough.

Bathing suits and pants designed for "thicker" guys have all found me on Instagram. I've also said yes and opted for expedited shipping to overnight "the only serum my aging, sun-spotted skin will ever need."

But I get a little confused when teased with "The Cutest Bras For Women Over Fifty."

I am over fifty, and I'm proud to say, I am not a man who needs a bra.

And truth be told, the bras are not that cute. They're fine, but I'm not sure why the five women in the ad are so excited about these bras. Admittedly, it's not an area of expertise I can claim on my LinkedIn profile, but I've seen cuter bras on QVC while flipping through the channels at 1:00 a.m. Much how like dogs watch *Bluey,* QVC can lull me into a happy stupor. I am mesmerized watching Isaac Mizrahi promise me that melon is the only color I need for summer. In a fleeting moment, I wish I was that person who could be ready for anything with just a pima cotton t-shirt in a soft shade of cantaloupe.

Occasionally, the algorithm shows concern that I might be prone to osteoporosis. I assume that's prompted by my click-through to a revolutionary bra-like garment proven to correct my posture. Yoga has put me on posture alert. I'm worried about that upper-body slump I often see in the checkout line at Citarella's.

In addition to cute bras and corrective undergarments, I get lots of offers for Chico's-style separates. Bold colors. Big prints. Sassy gal stuff. Carefully considering an ad for caftans, I understand the tranquil mindset inspired by these breezy garments.

I'm curious. No—I'm stymied.

Why do "they" think I'm a woman?

Is this predictive analytics at work?

Am I on my way to becoming a woman?

I need to know: *Why am I getting the same ads as Joy Behar and Kathy Bates?*

And then I wonder, *Why am I not perceived to be a woman with a little more sophistication? Why is there no outreach from La Perla? Tory Burch? St. John Knits? At the very least Eileen Fisher?*

Hello, rabbit hole! Rabbits make room! Here I come.

Possible reasons the internet thinks I need a bra:

1. I ordered a few baking tools and a couple of candles. But hey, I can't be the first guy to place an order at Williams Sonoma.
2. I ordered a vacuum cleaner. Let's hope our algorithms have moved beyond the prescriptive gender-assigned chores of a binary world.

Then I check my search history. Aha! Here's a list of things I've googled that are surely common in the search histories of women over fifty:

- Omar Sharif
- Ronan Farrow
- Mannix
- Michael Bublé
- Olympic ice skating
- Oprah
- Prince Harry
- Daniel Craig
- Barry Manilow
- Vital Proteins
- Richard Marx
- Jon Bon Jovi
- Linda Evans
- The Mandrell Sisters
- Josh Groban

Yes—I watched a Josh Groban video on YouTube. Once! I was curious: *Who* is this guy's audience? Who comes home from work and punches in Josh Groban on Spotify? I think I watched a performance on *The Ellen Show*. I get it—he's the new Barry Manilow. Sweeping and swelling promises of love best served with a buttery chardonnay and a Yankee Candle.

To check that assessment, I click on a clip from a Barry concert in London, maybe at Royal Albert Hall. Maybe in the early 80s.

I'm feeling very Margaret Meade–ish. I'm deep in the jungle of the internet, carefully studying a species of woman that is almost invisible in the wild. They swoon over men with tenor tendencies. They lose their shit over vocal gladiators who slay adult contemporary ballads. Their playlist is the musical equivalent of a fat-free diet: all romance and no sex.

Manilow's audience is filled with women who look like Hillary Clinton at different ages and stages throughout her life. Many of them are fresh from the office, rockin' it in business suits. When Barry hits the first few chords of "Weekend in New England," these women are close to rapture. There are no drugs at this concert. They aren't tanked or stoned. They don't have poppers in their Dooney & Bourke bags. Maybe they had a glass of wine with their shepherd's pie before the show, but these women are high on Barry. They are tripping on pure human ecstasy.

And I am jealous.

Observing them from a distance of time and space, I draw conclusions based solely on unsubstantiated assumptions. Marketers are very good at making their opinions sound like facts. If I were to construct an archetype persona of a Barry consumer, it might look like this:

- Very organized cabinets and drawers. Never have to spend ninety minutes looking for their social security card.
- They go through life with a very tight group of gal pals.
- Their lives might not be big, but they are the heart of their small world.
- Believe *The Great British Baking Show* really is better than sex.
- Will never go to St. Bart's or Paris Fashion Week, and they don't care.
- They never give up a week of cheesy biscuits to do a juice cleanse.
- Never, ever leave home without a little chocolate tucked away in their very sensible purse.
- A happy tribe of easy-listening fans.
- Click-on links to toffee pudding and comfortable sandals.
- They always say yes to a key lime pie.

I'm not them. I have a talent for saying no. For many years, I was the anomaly who could smoke just one cigarette a day. I stepped out into the night around 11:00 p.m. and mindfully enjoyed every last drag of an American Spirit (blue box). But that was it. I didn't want to be a "smoker"—I wanted to be a person who had a daily cigarette even if that one cigarette was as addictive as smoking a pack a day. When I say no to key lime pie, another brownie, or midweek cocktails, some people see it as virtue signaling. Underneath the control, I fantasize about all the cigarettes, sweets, and treats I haven't enjoyed. The martinis that never got stirred. The big bowl of pasta that was overruled by broiled salmon. I envy Barry's Fanilows and their exuberant embrace of a yes life. They know they can't dance, but that doesn't stop them.

At Barry's concert, they are a joyful collective of dancing queens sharing in an extended easy-listening sing-along.

The women who love Barry Manilow, Josh Groban, and Michael Bublé are exuberant about lots of things, big and small. They'd surely click on an ad for "cute bras."

I'm a bit envious of this woman the internet thinks I am. I want to be exuberant. I like being exuberant. Not all the time, but once in a while.

Perhaps I've lost my capacity for exuberance?

No. I'm exuberant when I travel. Once the packing is done. And then again when I'm back home.

I'm exuberant about sweaters. In my next life, I will own a sweater shop. Just sweaters. No shirts. No pants. No shoes. Just shelves and shelves of sweaters. I won't sell you a sweater, I will find the sweater that wants you to wear it. I'll be more like an art curator, helping you build a very personal knitwear collection.

I was exuberant about running. Clocking forty to forty-five miles a week was easy. Even in extreme heat or driving snow, it was exhilarating. The bonus: I could indulge my exuberance for big bowls of cheesy pasta.

Exuberance is a big emotion, but it doesn't require a huge moment.

It can play out in small ways: a newfound passion for woodworking, pickleball, cooking, paddleboarding, cartooning, golf, or surfing. Recently, I was taught a new card game: Fruit Cocktail. I *cannot* wait to play it again. Even if you have a definitive lead going into the final hand, it's a game that's very much alive until the last card is played.

I hadn't expected exuberance in a yoga class. It didn't see it coming.

But there it was: A pose I found challenging was suddenly accessible and effortless. Instead of collapsing onto my hip, I floated up into a buoyant and wobble-free Warrior 3. I was perfectly balanced with newfound strength and lift—an unexpected lightness of being.

Maybe my teacher noticed. Maybe not. It didn't matter.

There's the trick; you may not always know your destination until you get there. A surprising accomplishment can reward us with a sly sense of emotional exuberance.

My friend, Kathryn, who knows a thing or two about everything, advised me how to rewrite the algorithm that's driving my digital feed. The morning after a few searches for men's workout gear, I woke up to an offer for Granite Male and a veiled promise that my lady would be very, very happy. For a brief moment, my "cute bra" alter-ego gal was both taken aback but equally titillated.

Instead of prompts for sassy sandals or a new poncho, I was being lured into a seedy dialogue with the promise of a rock-hard joystick attached to a testosterone-juiced new me. I never clicked on Granite Male. I knew the game. I'd be sucked into the world of stuff for men over fifty. Waiting for me behind the paywall was a jacked-up new life. My screen would be pumping out offers for Harley Davidson gear, Ed Hardy cuffs, sassy shirts from a Paul Fredrick catalog, and butt-lifting underwear.

As we've seen before in this book, just like in life, digressions are irresistible. And just like life, this book thing is harder than I want it to be.

Do I bail?

No—what the hell am I going to do with 218 pages that add up to nothing. I don't want a file on my desktop labeled "Unfinished stuff." I do not want to be a work in progress.

Life is not a linear process. Neither is writing. It's like driving around Boston without GPS. You'll eventually get where you're going, but you can't be sure you'll be there on time. Lucky for you and me, there's no ticking clock. No matter where you are in life, you still have time to get to the next version of you. But drive carefully; if you go too fast, you may miss the turn you're looking for.

"WHEN CAN I GET FAT?"

I've asked myself this question many times. Quite often, friends note the expansive tendencies that inevitably come with age. One day, driving home from yoga, I answer a call from my friend, Jake. Even if we only connect twice a year, whenever we talk, he feels like a soulmate. He skips hello and gets right to the point.

"I want to get fat. I'm not kidding."

"If you were fat, you wouldn't be hot. And you like being hot."

"I'd still be hot. I wouldn't be *as* hot."

"No, you wouldn't be hot. You'd be beefy."

"You think I'm hot. Cool."

"Only because you're straight. If you were gay, you'd be a show-queen."

"I'm on my way to the gym and I gotta tell you, there's ten things I'd rather be doing."

"Just watch your carbs…."

Jake's voice bellows through the phone. "I'm tired of watching carbs…I mean, who gives a shit if I'm fat or not?"

"I care. I can't be friends with you if you develop carb-face."

"You mean you'll only be friends with attractive people?"

"No. Just you. I can't be friends with you if you're chubby. It's fine if you're beefy but you can't be chubby."

I'm in line behind two guys at Jack's Coffee in Amagansett. That's two guys. Early thirties. I watch them eyeing the muffins. They exchange conspiratorial smiles.

One says to the other, "Split one?"

Does no one eat a whole muffin anymore?

Guys are the new girls, I almost said out loud. And these two…these top-knots would burn me with hot lattes for even thinking in such a binary way.

Instagram is a showcase for mano-rexia. Just as women were always trapped by a beauty standard, guys now count, judge, weigh in, track BMI, preen, and pose. They sometimes love themselves too much and sometimes hate themselves for no reason. Thankfully, many people embrace the liberation and freedom of body-positivity, but as evidenced in recent body image statistics, very few people experience weight gain without apology or remorse.

I am well aware of the benefits that come with maintaining a healthy diet and healthy weight. I carry a healthy degree of vanity. I never want to look in the mirror and see a favorite sweater squeezing me like cashmere sausage casing. As my metabolism slows to a crawl, I say no more often than yes to everything I love. Pasta has become my enemy. Scones are evil. Fries are a delicious pest.

My ear returns to my phone. Jake builds his case.

"John Travolta got fat. Matt Damon and Vince Vaughn got hefty. DiCaprio is squishy. Clooney is Spanxed onto the red carpet. At what point can I relax and enjoy a Manhattan and a ramekin of chips every night before dinner just like my dad did? Huh? No, really—when? When can I say, 'Enough! I already worked out twice this week!'"

I have questions, too, but he keeps going.

"When can I say, 'I need to get a new belt' instead of salivating over success stories featured on the CoolSculpting website?"

"Dude—would you really pay to have your fat frozen?"

"It's a couple of grand."

"You called them—?"

"Fuck, yeah, I called. If I didn't have two college tuitions facing me in ten years, I'd have my gut sucked dry."

Every brand has a visual component. Product and package design are flash communicators about whether a brand is "for me." Artisanal and luxury products have a specific set of visual cues. Typically, their graphics are imperfect, cuing the handmade promise of small-batch brands. Science-based brands have their own set of markers, usually designed to reassure efficacy, purity, and product safety. Brands designed for kids and teens have their decidedly different, more colorful graphic languages, often sending visual dog whistles seen only by these younger consumers. There are design cues that tee up sophistication, ruggedness, trust, excitement, and competence.

When it comes to human brands, sleek, sexy, and confident will always attract more attention than schlumpy and frumpy. Since we can't walk naked into the streets, fashion has been our toolbox for creating our real-life avatar—an exercise in self-actualization. We are our own billboards, walking through life, letting people know how we want to be seen. Conversely, there's also the antifashion, screw-the-status-quo people. Their "who cares what people think?" antistyle becomes its own brand of I-don't-care cool—carefully designed to broadcast their rebellious independence or eccentric edge.

But that's not me. Like most people, I benefit from grooming.

I'm not man-orexic, but without a few guardrails in place, I'd be twice the man I am today.

I'm not getting fat this year. And probably not next year. But I promise, at some point, I'm going to say yes to all of my nos: cheese, nightly cocktails, chips, pizza Fridays, and big tubs of popcorn every time I nestle into the dark of a movie theater. I will reduce the number of hours I spend in exercise mode. But not just yet. I'm not comfortable seeing photos of myself looking twenty-five years older than I am in my head. I'm certainly not ready to start seeing pictures in which I'm twenty-five pounds heavier than I am now. Not yet, anyway.

Someday.

Promise.

Today, I'm not quite ready to look like the typical class of 1978.

Vitamin O and other drugs can curb my food intake, but I don't want an appetite lobotomy.

There's a restaurant near us that serves short-rib mac 'n' cheese. It's on my to-do list for this year. In order to really enjoy it, I have to set it up for success. I'll be a pound or two below my norm. I'll do a yoga class. Then I'll run eight miles. We'll head out to an early dinner. I'm not quite on early-bird time yet, which should now be called Viagra Standard Time. Isn't dinner what happens while men of the khaki generation wait for the little blue pill to kick in? Or is it kick up?

Here's the scene I imagine: A magic-hour sunset will paint the restaurant with a warm glow. I'll order my martini and that short-rib mac 'n' cheese. I'll savor every last bite.

To whomever's with me, I'll say, "No, you cannot have a taste."

I feel it. It's almost time. My next version of me is going to say yes more than no.

"Yes, I'm getting older."

"Yes, fighting nature is an unwinnable war."

"Yes, I would like a bourbon Manhattan in the dead of winter while we watch *Project Runway*."

"Yes, I have put on a little weight." Nine pounds over the last decade, to be exact.

It's my destiny. It's either that or a perpetual state of longing. Besides, what is my natural vibe? In general, am I a yes or a no guy? Am I so concerned about image that I live in a constant state of fear of who I am naturally?

I've never had fun with someone who counts their carrots. They make me nervous. Sure, they can tuck their shirt into their pants, but they never smile when they say "cheese."

"Do you ever do this brand shit on yourself?"

I come back to this question. Brand tools are designed to provide clarity, focus, and direction. They're not magic. They simply provide a path for decision making.

I pause.

I reflect.

My hands leave the keyboard. My shoulders relax. My eyes leave the screen and look out the window. It's not a poetic moment. But it's quiet. I can hear my own thoughts. I ask myself, "Now what?" But it's less of a question. "Now what?" sounds like the starter gun at the start of a race. I have my mandates:

- Live the life I have now. Not the one I had or never had.
- Create a steady stream of fresh answers to "What's new?"
- Keep a list of new things to see, read, watch, and learn. Rather than a to-do or bucket list, I view it as my list of possibilities.
- A few doses of urgency would be welcome. Turn "one day" into today!
- Cultivate new situational friends. Invite a fellow yogi over for dinner.
- Master the art of chitchat. I can talk to anybody, but I still don't always connect.
- Maximize bone-marrow friends.
- Find activities and interests that prompt exuberance.
- Aspire to be Andy-happy.
- Get comfortable with nothingness.
- Find my next something.
- Surprise myself.
- Do a fashion check.
- Eat cheese in moderation.
- Walk, just for the hell of it.
- Write. Even if the writing has no purpose, it definitely gets shit out of my head.
- Develop a good feedback loop.
- Be mindful of first impressions. Be sure this book doesn't make me look like an ass.
- Sleep more. Worry less.
- Create a cul-de-sac life.
- Remember, everybody was somebody.
- Even when you retire, don't ever be finished.

It's a lot. Even if I don't get to everything, even just hitting 30 percent of this list will get me to a new me.

And one more thing:

We are living in the age of unenlightenment. We are bombarded with a daily deluge of news, opinion, and marketing content. It's all aggressive. It's frantic. Now and then, do a pop-culture cleanse. Turn everything off. Watch nothing. Hear nothing. Spend an entire weekend listening to your own thoughts. Get to know what you think and feel. A good dose of quiet will quiet the agitation of the outside world.

It's how yoga begins and how the class ends. Everything is loud and clear in the quiet.

"RAY SEEMS HAPPY."

I stop at Carissa's for a coffee. I much prefer Jack's Coffee, but, let's be honest, I'm there for the chocolate croissant.

"Can I warm that for you?"

"Nope. But thanks."

I like to bite through chocolate. I'm in the car, savoring my first hit of the dark cacao. Incoming call. An unknown number always worries me, but I answer it anyway.

"Norton!"

"Yeah?"

"You don't know who this is, do you?"

"Nope."

I hate this game. Every now and then, people from your past see you on Facebook and spontaneously reach out.

This is Los Angeles 1993 calling.

We do the "What about…?" mini update on everyone who made up the group of "us" in a former lifetime. It's that tightly knit group of people you assumed would be with you forever, but then you graduate, move, quit, change, or don't change. And then one day, you don't really know each other anymore.

"You know, I see Ray on Facebook. I don't check it as much, but when I take a look, I always see something from Ray."

"Houses. He takes pictures of houses while walking around Los Angeles."

"Walking in Los Angeles. Sounds like a book."

"That's how he lost weight!"

"Well, he had to. After his heart thing."

"Oh, right. But he seems happy."

"Yeah. Ray does seem happy. Or he knows how to look happy on Facebook."

Consumers are driven by a constant craving for something new. Fresh ideas are the lifeblood of marketing. To compete successfully with the never-ending deluge of new products, marketers must focus their dollars on the consumer for whom their product was designed. My students at Parsons hear this constant refrain throughout the semester, "You can't sell every 'thing' to everybody."

Decisions must be made.

Positioning statements are crafted to cement the "who" and "why" of your marketing plan. A positioning statement identifies the target consumer, what they want or need, and the unique difference your product brings to their life.

Here's a standard format for a positioning statement:

For [ideal consumer] **who** [has this challenge], **our** [product name] **is a** [product category] **that provides** [key benefit and reason to buy]. **Unlike** [the competition or alternative], **our product** [Unique Selling Proposition (USP)].

Positioning statements are not supposed to be clever. They require concise, precise, simple, and exacting language.

Your positioning statement is an antidote to being overwhelmed by choices, options, and ideas. It creates the bull's-eye for your budget.

It sets your key objective for the short term, eliminating the noise of possibilities.

My friend Ray is passionate about three things: He's a game freak (analog or digital), a voracious reader (fiction and nonfiction), and a movie freak (in any genre). I think, on average, Ray reads over 200 books and somehow sees about 150 movies each year. Ray retains everything he sees and reads, which helped him win both *Jeopardy!* and *Win Ben Stein's Money*.

When Ray turned fifty, he made a pact with himself: maintain youthful energy and relevance. As a single gay man without children, Ray realized he needed to actively cultivate friendships with younger people. Boomers spent the last few decades of the twentieth century joking about befuddled parents not knowing how to program the VCR. Ray had a nightmare image of himself unable to engage with the future of our digitally designed world. Young people are fearless—they're ravenous for what's new. Younger people provide a vital connection to next-gen technology and contemporary culture.

When it came to "gaming," Ray was ahead of the curve. Ray was a very early adopter of video games, which skewed younger than Ray's immediate world. He would hide away for an entire weekend playing video games. Who did that? Certainly no one we knew. Wasn't gaming the domain of weird, awkward boys struggling through their teen years?

Ray started reviewing games for industry blogs, which gave him access to the latest games and a forum for his very confident opinions. Many of us didn't recognize that Ray's frontier spirit positioned him at the edge of the gaming explosion.

"Really, Ray? Is this worth your time?"

As Ray was diving deep into his new passion, he saw the trap: Without young people in his life, without their rabid quest for what's next, it would be game over.

What's an aging gamer to do if your contemporaries don't want to stay home and play?

Ray strategized. He got creative.

Cultivating a new pack of gamers was easier than he thought it would be. Younger people, with their unlimited energy and sometimes limited budgets, love weekend game-a-thons. He dove into meetup.com. In LA, meetup.com led him to binge gaming nights. When he traveled for business, rather than sit in a hotel room, Ray would connect with gamers everywhere he went. In these groups, Ray's enthusiasm for games is what defined him. His gaming prowess made him cool. Like a seasoned musician or surfer, it's not your age that defines you, it's that thing you do.

In less than a year, Ray's apartment was filled with new friends, most of them half his age. They idolized Ray's knowledge and intensity. They learned from Ray's gaming skills and strategies. They became better gamers because of Ray. They shared his enthusiasm and energy. When they looked at Ray, they didn't see an old guy. They saw a fellow gamer. An awesome player.

And a bud.

Without knowing it, Ray had lived out a perfectly executed positioning statement. He had a mission (meet younger people), a goal (have younger energy in my life), and a relevant USP (Unique Selling Proposition—awesome game player). If Ray had actually formalized a position statement, it may have read like this:

For game night enthusiasts **who** are really in it to win it, **my** playfully competitive nature **is an** energizing force **that provides** a seriously fun edge to game nights. **Unlike** most game players you know, **I am** a former *Jeopardy* champion.

There is no mention of age. Ray is simply and clearly focused on people with a love of games. It's social, but serious.

Ray's positioning statement is as specific as it needs to be; it targets people who appreciate his skill level and welcome serious competition.

A year after putting himself in the market, so to speak, Ray's KPIs (Key Performance Indicators) were impressive.

In business terms, he exceeded his goals.

On Thanksgiving, he went to a Friendsgiving dinner. Ray had a lot to be thankful for: He was seated at a table surrounded by younger people, all of whom he'd met within the previous twelve months. As he marches toward sixty, there's a big, fun, playful world out there that revolves around Ray. Mission accomplished.

"What about you, Norton? What's new with you? Still running?"

"Yoga. I replaced running with yoga."

"Did the knees finally give out?"

"No, I just stopped running one day. Maybe just in time."

"Hey, Norton, next time you're in LA, can we do a hearts night?"

"You know, yeah—let's."

"Great."

"But we have to start much earlier, and there can't be any cheese."

"Who eats cheese anymore?"

What's the point of this call?

"I'm really glad I answered the phone. What made you call out of the blue?"

"I was just talking about you. I always said, 'Given the amount of time we spent around each other, I never really felt like I knew you.' I liked you. But you were always sort of 'CIA.'"

"I get that a lot."

"You were never as funny as your writing."

"I get that a lot too."

"You know what else was weird about you? That you ran *and* smoked."

"It wasn't weird if you were me. I enjoyed both in equal measure."

Why is he calling me? I actually don't want to know.

"Hey, I've gotta jump. I've got a Zoom in five."

"Oh. Okay. Hearts night. Next time."

"Say hi to Ray."

"Hey, Norton, still writing at all?"

"No. Nope."

How do you justify this lie? you might be thinking.

This is a conversation with my past. This person knows me as a writer. Knew me. A writer in the business of screenwriting. What you're reading is being written for me. There is no commercial intent, expectation, or requirement. I don't have to get an agent excited. No junior development exec will do coverage on this book. No creative VP will peruse a one-page recap while a masseur kneads their back and massages their ego. No one has to like it, love it, hate it, dismiss it, or decide if it has any A-list appeal or indie-cred.

Even though I kept this book a secret, it felt great to at least have an inside-voice answer to "What's new with you?"

"I BLAME EVERYTHING ON HILLARY CLINTON!"

In so many words, I hear this a lot. I even heard it the day after forty-five became forty-seven.

"Everything?! Hillary is the root cause of everything that bothers you?"

It was one of those many days when we woke up to yet another offensive, outrageous, egregious, or illegal shenanigans of the first Trump presidency. During those "WTF?" years, as my fellow yogis drifted toward their cars, there was a need to give voice to the fury pounding inside their heads. No amount of "namaste" could calm those mornings.

"Trying to bribe Ukraine?!"

"No reason not to believe Putin?"

"Bleach? He can't be that dumb!"

"Very fine people… What's next—a national holiday for David Duke's birthday?"

I start the car. I check my phone. A friend, whose texts I call *The Daily Crazy*, sends three links to *WAPO*, *Bloomberg*, and *WSJ* news stories and adds this: "I blame Hillary for everything. It's all because of her."

Stop it. Stop hating Hillary. Just stop it!

Right now, much of our identity is being forged through our political opinion. We underscore our position with a squinty-eyed look that says, "I know what I'm talking about!"

It's been said that you are what you eat. Or that clothes make the man. Not anymore. Now, we are what we opine. It's as if everyone is camera-ready with their personal take on today's breaking news. Even though you've got a lightning-hot insight on the situation, CNN is not going to cut away from Jake Tapper to get your take on the day's crazy headline. Not only has Trump completely disrupted our democracy, he's stolen 75 percent of my me time. How can I possibly search my soul and reimagine my future now that I'm required to analyze the latest RCP polls before going out to dinner?

Not too long ago, if you were at a dinner party with a challenging mix of people, somebody would rescue the conversation with a chitchat starter. You know chitchat starters. They go something like this: "If you could murder one person—and it wouldn't be a crime or a sin—who would you kill? And how?"

Chitchat starters work. They helped me through many business dinners. They provide a forum for creativity, humor, and personal philosophy. They often reveal a person's true character and core beliefs. And people listen. They listen, check their reaction, and then respond—which, by the way, is the traditional structure of a conversation.

Now that we all sound media trained and step into the world fully armed with a point of view, I don't hear "umm" as much. We get right to it with "The way I see it…", "For me…", and "If you really think about it, if you boil it down…", which carries a subtle implication that no one else at the table has a thought with any rigor or merit behind it.

The mood doesn't allow for fun chitchat starters anymore. Nothing designed to provoke our imaginations. Too many conversations revolve around Donald Trump. I am now prepped with what I call "confrontation starters":

Who are your two least favorite Democrats?

Who are your two least favorite Republicans?

Who's worse: Donnie 2 or MTG?

On the other side, they're trashing AOC, Shifty Schiff, Crazy Nancy, and everybody's favorite nasty woman, Hillary.

Thank Hillary Clinton for elevating "deplorable" in our collective consciousness. Many say that was her big mistake. I say her biggest mistake was not doubling down on "deplorable" and holding everyone accountable for the true costs of racism, misogyny, bigotry, and a culture built on lies. It's deplorable that bullying became a campaign norm. Not all, and maybe not most, but many people who serve and support Tweety Don are fueled by hate, and, in any form, that's deplorable. So, if the word fits, put it on a t-shirt and wear it proudly.

Speaking of Hillary—as people often do—she is cited by many as their least favorite Democrat. Hillary just drives people crazy—Republicans and Democrats alike. Men and women! Hillary has been under our skin for decades.

In addition to forfeiting the deplorable conversation, here's a list of Hillary's most popular mistakes:

1. The private email server
2. Staying with Bill
3. Staying loyal to Huma
4. Feeling entitled
5. Picking Tim Kaine as her VP
6. Not going to Michigan and Wisconsin
7. Being unlikable
8. The cookie comment
9. Don't forget Benghazi
10. And thinking she was "all that" when it came to health care

Okay, Hillary didn't get to be one of our best presidents ever, but she will never be forgotten. I'm sure fifty years from now, the Broadway musical, *Hillary!*, will be bigger than *Evita*. Bigger than *Hamilton*. Hillary will be that tragic, feisty, and misunderstood character whose defiant power anthem creates the next Patti LuPone.

Hillary-hating was an easy way out of 2016. Dump all the blame on her for not visiting Wisconsin and Michigan. That assumption is silly. If Hillary had gone to Michigan, do we know for sure she would have carried the state? Is there any empirical proof that seventy thousand people in Wisconsin and Michigan would have switched their vote from Trump to Hillary if she had swung by their state fair and chowed down on a corn dog?

You can say hubris tripped up Hillary and her campaign staff. From a marketing perspective, perhaps they made the mistake of taking their existing customers for granted. You never do that. Marketers know that it's much more efficient to maintain your current customer with just a little love. If you lose them, winning them back costs even more time and money. How and why the decision was made to skip those key states, we don't know. Were they overconfident or chasing a bad strategy? We can have an opinion, but we can't act like we *know*. There are people who didn't vote at all. People who Jill Stein–ed the vote count. People who opted for Trump. I blame all those voters much more than I blame Hillary.

Blaming it all on Hillary ignores the reality that she had more working against her than any candidate in history: Putin, Comey, Russians, Julian Assange, men, women, bots, trolls, Anthony Weiner, and pneumonia. People say she should never have been the candidate because she's always been unlikable. I sat at a dinner party where an informed, intelligent, sixty-something woman defiantly and proudly said, "I know Hillary is the best-qualified candidate and she'd make a great president, but I just don't like her so I can't vote for her."

Voting is how we hire our president. When you vote, you are not selecting new pledges for your sorority.

Do I wish Hillary won? Yes. Do I think she made mistakes? Of course. Every candidate makes mistakes. We all make mistakes. The selection of Tim Kaine as her running mate was a bigger mistake than not visiting Wisconsin. Choosing the senator from Virginia as her VP was a strategic decision rather than a daring move. The "who'd've thunk" enthusiasm for Donald Trump was a neon sign pointing at an electorate that was craving disruption. This hunger for an outsider was also evident in the candidacy of Bernie Sanders. With Hillary, the Democrats had a woman at the top of the ticket—that's a big, bold change. But Clinton and Kaine were not stronger together. She and Tim Kaine looked like a presidential ticket from the twentieth century rather than a visionary political brand for the twenty-first century.

If I were her strategist, I would have marched Hillary onto *The Howard Stern Show* before the election. When she finally went on Howard's show in 2019, he unleashed the Hillary we never saw in candidate

Hillary. Howard is a brilliant interviewer. He would have prompted the unguarded "moment" Hillary needed to get an additional seventy thousand people to like her. Really like her.

I get lost wanting to rewrite history.

"If only…."

"If only this…if only that…if only so many things."

"If Hillary had won, would we still hate her?"

It's sad to say…but probably. Hating Hillary seems to be a sport on the verge of having a national competition. We have a desperate need for outrage in our lives, and Hillary has always been a natural resource for mining fury. If she had a scent, it would be called Vitriol. I do not remember people hating on Al Gore or John Kerry when they lost their equally consequential elections. People were disappointed—yes. Sad? Without question. In fact, Gore's loss was worse than Hillary's. Hillary's loss gave us Trump. The assault on our democracy is alarming. But if Gore had been president, we'd be in climate control rather than climate crisis. We may have never had a war in Afghanistan. Maybe 9/11 wouldn't have happened. How much of twenty-first-century history would have been rewritten with Gore sitting in the White House? With Gore, we blame Florida. With Kerry, we blame the U-boat video. With Hillary, we blame Hillary. In 2016, the pantsuit stood alone.

In the future, we will thank Hillary. Ironically, her greatest contribution to history might just be losing the election. I'll cop to it—I never knew democracy was such a fragile construct. I never thought our hard-won rights could be reversed with the stroke of a sharpie. I never imagined that one election could dramatically change the promise of America. Donald's Operation Tweetstorm is the text version of an AK-47, assaulting our image as "the land of the free and the home of the brave." His regime obliterates the truth on a daily basis. His petulant tirades blunt the criticism of his fellow Republicans.

The reason we can't stop talking about Hillary is because her loss shattered our individual and collective worlds. It's now on us to fix this mess, and that means we can't be complacent or passive. We want our big, grandstanding opinions to save us. Blaming Hillary makes us feel better. It gives us a false sense of power. One little trip to Michigan would have fixed everything. Sadly, we want life to be that easy. If Hillary had won, we would have settled right back into our lives, charging forward over the cracks that had already weakened the foundation of our democracy. We'd still be blind to the systemic racism that shaped this country from day one. We'd never hear the painful anger rooted in our "have and have-not economy." Sooner or later, a Trump-like moment was coming.

Democracy only works if you work at it. Democracy was on thin ice, but we didn't see it until Hillary failed to break the glass ceiling. On that night, we all started singing, "Bye, Bye, Miss American Pie."

I often think of the opening line from *The Way We Were*. As the camera moves in close on Hubbell Gardiner, portrayed with perfect, privileged blondeness by Robert Redford, a voiceover observes, "In a way he was like the country he lived in; everything came too easily to him. But at least he knew it."

Maybe we thought life, liberty, and the pursuit of happiness was easier than it really is. Maybe we were all a little bit like Hubbell Gardiner, unaware of the dangers percolating in the world. Yes—we have Hillary to thank for Trump, but perhaps we also have to thank her for our newfound commitment to truth, justice, and the American way.

Obviously, I don't hate Hillary, but if this book doesn't get decent reviews or doesn't sell enough copies to get a second printing, I will blame Hillary. Why not? It's all her fault, right? In fact, should I blame her for Bradley Cooper not winning best actor for *A Star Is Born*? I have no other explanation for why he didn't win. As talented as Rami Malek is, impersonations should not win Oscars. And, certainly, impersonations should not win presidential elections.

Thanks to all this shit I've learned at yoga, I don't wrestle with the past. My mistakes. The roads not taken. History cannot be rewritten. Yesterday is done.

This new me confounds me sometimes. We're still getting to know each other. New me is much more accepting than the old me. I wake up ChatGPT with a simple prompt: "Is yoga bliss real?"

"Yoga bliss" typically refers to the deep sense of peace, contentment, and joy that can arise during or after a yoga practice. It's not a formal or technical term, but rather a common phrase used to describe the positive emotional and physical state people often experience when practicing yoga regularly.

Key Aspects of "Yoga Bliss":

Mental calm: A quiet, focused mind from practices like breathwork and meditation.

Emotional balance: Feeling centered, grounded, and emotionally stable.

Whatever bliss I get from yoga, it's under attack the minute I leave the studio. But through yoga, I've developed the emotional muscle to maintain command of my day.

Here's one last chitchat starter: if you could change one moment in history, what would it be?

Now I know that beliefs aren't facts, but if I could rewrite history, I truly believe that President Hillary would have at least given bliss a chance.

LIVING THE CHANGE

"AFTER SIXTY..."

"Oh—hey—hi..."

That's my slightly startled acknowledgement of a client actually calling rather than texting to assess my availability for a Teams meeting.

"Good weekend?" I ask my client. As you do on a Monday morning.

"No."

How often do you hear anything other than "amazing" or "total chill"? Who admits to a bad weekend?

"Oh—sorry. Everything OK?"

"Well, no. I turned sixty."

Get client "Established 1963" vintage-style T-shirt on Etsy.

"Oh. Didn't know. Happy birthday!"

"Happy? Sixty?"

"It feels old and odd, but it can be a great decade."

"You'll have to tell me about it sometime. I sent out a meeting invite, but you're the only one who hasn't responded."

"Oh sorry, I didn't see it. When? Yesterday?"

"No. About an hour ago."

"Oh, I was in yoga."

"Yoga? You don't seem like you do yoga."

"Oh...not sure what that means."

"My neighbor does yoga and he's boring."

"Well, lots of interesting people do yoga. Sting does yoga."

"Sting is boring."

"Ryan Gosling does yoga."

"If he wasn't hot, he'd be boring."

"Jennifer Aniston."

"I was never a *Friends* fan."

This newly minted sixty-year-old sure is a grumpy old man.

"Yoga would be a great birthday gift to give yourself."

"Can you get on the call at one?"

"Yes. See you then."

Who doesn't love a good list? I can't resist any "Ten Best..." or "Where Are They Now?" list that pops up on my iPhone. I'll always click on "People You Didn't Know Were Gay" but always wonder, "Who didn't know that Jane Lynch and Neil Patrick Harris are gay?!" So, here's my list of things that I kind-of knew but didn't *really* know until I turned sixty, which, coincidentally, is when I started up with yoga again.

1. *The Godfather* is good, but it's not the greatest movie of all time. It's not. And arguing about it makes you look old.
2. Under no circumstance should you ever get your picture taken next to someone who is twenty-seven, thirty-two, or even forty-four years old. Even in the best light, standing next to them, your skin tone looks gray, your jawline is an undefined blur, and your hair does, in fact, look dull and listless. You will then waste forty-eight hours looking in the mirror trying to convince yourself that it's just a really bad photo. It isn't. You will never again look like the picture you hold in your head. You're old. And that's a good thing with its own advantages. It's just not photogenic.
3. Close proximity to tight skin can induce a revitalizing euphoria, but don't think you can still rock out at Coachella.
4. High school never ends. People love cliques. And someone always feels left out.
5. Time doesn't fly, it takes the Concorde.
6. Extreme hair care is a waste of money.

7. Getting older is expensive. Particularly if you want nice teeth and even-toned skin.
8. Netflix is the greatest invention of our time. It's the digital equivalent of fire. And now you love staying home.
9. The bucket list is bullshit. You can tell because it made a really, really bad movie.
10. You might fart without warning.
11. If you're over forty-five and male, don't let your coworkers see your legs. If you're at a national sales meeting in Cabo—no shorts. I saw a boss—straight—in a speedo. From that day forward, I could never take his questions or suggestions seriously.
12. Old friends can reawaken your soul. Unless they ask for money.
13. Elton John has always been awesome, even if you didn't know it at the time.
14. If you're the oldest person in a meeting, that's exactly who you are and who you'll always be every time you enter a conference room. You are older than the parents of most of the people who work with you.
15. Do not reference a story from the twentieth century unless you had some random make-out session with JFK Jr.
16. If you've started writing your first book, keep it a secret until you can tell people to come by your book signing.
17. You no longer give a crap about what people think.
18. You now have the freedom to be quirky.
19. You start living your own list. Even a stellar review in the *New York Times* can't make me see a movie I don't want to see.

The media landscape is littered with lists celebrating fame and fortune. "The Hundred Best…", "The Fifty Most Beautiful…", and "The Fifty Most Powerful…" But most people are never going to be on those lists.

This book will never put me on a "Best List" with John Irving, Colson Whitehead, Joyce Carol Oates, Donna Tartt, Hanya Yanagihara, David Sedaris, or Amor Towles. If that was my goal, I've written the wrong book. I did this for me. I wanted to get back to the "me" who woke up every day with a creative itch I couldn't wait to scratch.

Mission accomplished.

Hopefully, there's value in this book for you too.

My hope: Reading this book inspires a "shit list"—people who have read this book and found a new focus and energy. People who are now *the shit*.

Whether thirty years old or sixty years young, you can be on this list.

If you surprise yourself.

If you hit a wall and get your shit together.

If you find energizing and rewarding answers to "What's new?" and "Now what?", then you're on the list.

It may not turn you into a CNN hero, but this "shit list" will be equally impressive.

The list is a group of people who have succeeded beyond their circumstances and expectations. People who, with a little inspiration from this book, simply transform their mindset from "stuck" to "fast forward."

They're what every family, community, and workplace needs. In small ways, their newfound positivity transforms the world around them.

You don't have to do something extraordinary or unexpected. You're on the list if you use this book to find a greater sense of purpose and a more lasting sense of peace.

And, as we say in yoga, "Namaste."

"MIND THE MUDDLE."

SFX: Truck horn.

I'm in the car. In my mind, I'm replaying the class I just left. I need to remember what she said....

"Muddle!"

SFX: Rude truck horn. Simply rude.

In the rearview mirror I see a guy flipping me two fingers—one on each hand. *What's his problem?*

He swerves around me, barking insults that include "old," "ass," "mother f_____," and "twat."

Two things to note here:

One: "Old" seems unnecessary.

Two: "Twat" makes me laugh.

He could benefit from a few sessions of community yoga.

Cruising along on NY 27, en route to a chocolate bouchon, I continue with my playback of today's class.

"Commit to the pose, even before you move a muscle."

I recognize that I get ahead of myself. With everything.

"You know, in the London Underground, they say 'mind the gap'—that tricky space between the train and the platform. I say, 'mind the muddle.' It's the tricky space between intention and execution. If you're not focused on what you're doing, you'll be wobbling in the muddle. So, take this into Warrior 3."

I'm not in love with my Warrior 3.

I'm shockingly pleased when I'm perched on one leg, body floating parallel to the floor, and arms pointed toward Montauk.

I probably have a 35 percent success rate. I tend to sink onto my standing leg, but, most of the time, it's a mess, compromised by hesitancy and trepidation.

Doubt. It's a killer. And it gets amplified in the muddle—that's any time in life when you're rudderless and uncertain, like you're swimming in oatmeal. What's possible and probable turns to mush. When you're in a muddle, you don't know who you are, you don't know what you want or need.

Repetition breeds confidence. Familiarity eliminates uncertainty. As you move through your career, you get to the point when the meeting you're in today is your Groundhog Day. You could turn off the sound and still know what to say and when to say it. Confidence comes with knowing that nothing new is coming your way. No matter what it is, you've got this.

With major shifts, you're required to tackle a new set of firsts. It's been a while since you felt the thrill of a first kiss, first job, first promotion, first marriage, first kid, or a first prom. Now, the firsts aren't thrilling—they're terrifying.

First gray pubic hair.

First time you can't read the menu.

First time your dermatologist says, "...but it's something we characterize as precancerous."

Any incorporation of the word "cancer" is like hot sauce on your emotions.

Now, your "firsts" are fraught with fear or regrets.

Don't retreat to the shadows. It's imperative: Get comfortable feeling uncomfortable with your new firsts. You need the energy of "new" to combat the fear of "old."

These stories of a fearless pursuit of "new" helped rewire my brain:

A former nurse on a day I arrived early for a Vinyasa class

"I wasn't sure what I wanted to do with my time. I thought, 'What do I like to do?' I like to drive. Driving has always felt like freedom to me. So, I went to town and applied to be a school bus driver. Great hours. Easy schedule. And I make sure the kids on my bus have a good start and good end to the school day."

How awesome is she! She has the power to change the world every day.

A sparkly eyed man at Jack's Coffee after yoga

"The pack of you—you're in here every Thursday. You all do yoga?"

"Yeah. Sadly, next week, the new semester starts, and I start teaching on Thursday mornings."

"Ah—you teach? Yoga?"

"No. Branding and marketing. At Parsons."

"Ah—I was a college professor. Taught history."

"Do you miss the classroom?"

"Not even for a day. I had a plan. Teaching was a brain job. After thirty-five years, I wanted to do something with my hands. I retired and signed up for a class in sculpting. I'm seventy-three, and I just had my first gallery show."

He proves my point: Whether you're twenty or sixty years old, ten years is ten years. You can set the world on fire at any age.

After class with an executive on the eve of his retirement

"Lunch is on me," the executive says. "It's a thank-you."

"For what?"

"I took your advice. About retirement."

"Not retirement. Working differently."

"Exactly. Like you said, 'Everything you do, do differently.'"

"It's a way to give yourself fresh energy."

"When it came to charity, I never had time to do much more than write checks. And I was happy to do that…."

"As long as you do what you can…."

"Yeah, yeah, yeah. But now—with my *downshift*—everybody's been asking if we have big travel plans. I said to my wife, 'For the next five years, no more resorts, no more leading hotels of the world, no more glam adventures. Voluntourism! Let's go places where we can make a difference. Do good, and not just for stockholders.' We're on our way to help build orphanages in Africa."

"That's awesome!"

"It's different—good—packing my bags with a sense of purpose."

"Namaste!"

Who's more interesting, the person sitting on a beach in Anguilla, or the person who just returned from building an orphanage in Malawi?

None of these people called it quits. All of them had good reason to get up in the morning. They had something to do and something to say. They had stories to tell and stories worth repeating. They were not stuck in a muddle.

It's the personal stuff—relationships, friendships, jobs, and family—where we create our messy muddles. These relationships breed a fog of emotion.

People get stuck. They're confused by and afraid of the shit that clogs their brains. Our reputations precede us. You stand a chance of being the most interesting person in the room if you remember this: Your story of the past should never be more interesting than the story you're living now. The yogisms I've shared in this book can liberate you from your muddle.

For today, my pile of doubts is trounced by the sense of accomplishment that comes with finishing this chapter.

Onto the next.

No time to muddle around in the muddle.

"THAT WAS A LOT OF FASHION FOR A YOGA CLASS."

I'm at a light.

A text pings.

"That was a lot of fashion for a yoga class."

Somebody had to say it.

Every once in a while, there's that person.

Perhaps it's their first class.

Or perhaps they're visiting from Planet Instagram.

They arrive at the studio looking like their glam squad jumped into action around 5:45 a.m.

Makeup. Rings. Layers of cashmere and chunky knits.

That's a lot of fashion for yoga....

Yes—but we don't judge...out loud.

For the most part, yoga is a fashion-free zone.

Standing in prayer position, you are you. Your body. Your face. There is very little camouflage. Your canvas for self-expression is limited to a patterned legging and your choice of mat.

In downward dog, your hair goes upside down too.

There are some people—just a few—who can pull off "fashion" right up until their last day on earth. But that's not most people. Diane Keaton's genius isn't just her acting; it's her personal style. Diane has always skirted the traditional feminine image. Her inspired individuality created an indelible personal and professional brand.

Fashion seemed to be her protective shield, a way to resist Hollywood's expectations of what an actress should be. Interestingly, her outsider persona also became what every actor needs—a way to stand out. To become instantly recognizable and memorable. The clownlike volume of her fashion syncs with her quirky personality to create an iconic signature style. No matter what she wears, the designer is irrelevant. Diane wears it her way. Even when she wore Ralph Lauren, she gave the American romanticist an edge he could have never imagined for himself.

There are very few people who can transcend age and not wade into dangerous fashion territory. Try to imagine Mick Jagger or Steven Tyler without their rock-star drag. Close your eyes and picture them in khakis and a pique polo from Brooks Brothers. They wouldn't be rock stars. They'd just be two scrawny guys, fumbling over a Phil Collins oldie during karaoke night on a Caribbean cruise ship.

At a certain age, fashion no longer applies to you. That doesn't mean you forfeit style or surrender to a sexless image. But it does mean that if you buy something because it's "fun," then you're probably too old for the garment.

At the end of summer, when I return to campus, I *love* getting in the elevators jammed with the hard-core, notice-me fashion of many Parsons students. The edgier side of Chanel. Miu Miu. Gucci. Prada. It's all there, pressing into elevators packed with students and professors being lifted to their 12:10 p.m. classes. Thom Browne's witty and fantastic twists on classic design tropes look amazing on a twenty-year-old. If I was twenty, I'd be working four gigs so I could ravage the sale racks at Barney's (again, remember Barney's, sad face). I've stood in front of dressing room mirrors sadly accepting the truth:

ME

+

THOM BROWNE

=

An old Ken Doll who's eaten way too much cheese

At Parsons, I also see a constant parade of new street brands—clothes with bold, fun, energetic designs. And Parsons students wear it effortlessly. Perhaps there will come a day when I wear a drop-crotch pant for medical reasons, but right now, unstructured trousers and a big Supreme T-shirt would certainly compromise my authority in a client meeting.

Then there are the students who wear their creativity. They can't afford to shop the shops. These are the kids that rethink, redesign, rework, and remake recycled or vintage clothes. Their cool quotient isn't based on another designer's vision; they are an explosion of self-expression. They don't shop labels, price points, or the pages of *Vogue.* They play with fashion, exploring who they are and how they want to be seen. The image they create is a response to their world. Experimentation and pushing boundaries are their keys to finding the space they can comfortably call their own.

Fashion is a tool for discovery.

No matter what age or gender identity you declare, everyone should set aside a few hours to shop now and then. Old school. Brick-and-mortar. Try stuff on and face the mirror. You don't have to buy anything; look at trying on clothes as research. Don't limit yourself based on style or price. Standing in front of the dressing room mirror, wearing something out of your norm or beyond your reach may help you see the person you want to become. A new image can provide inspiration and aspiration. It can reveal the beauty in your new maturity. It can help you see who you've become. And, sometimes, it can be helpful to see who you're not. There are many versions of me in my head that will never be seen in public. They are ideas without practical application in my real world.

For me, "fashion" is now a spectator sport. That doesn't mean I'm not conscious and thoughtful about what I wear, unless you see me walking the dog.

At twenty-five, I rocked a Claude Montana leather jacket with billboard-wide shoulder pads. Even if, for some reason, that look cycled back into fashion, imagine how tragic I'd look if you saw me wearing it as I worked my way through the cracker aisle at Whole Foods.

Context must be considered when deciding who you want to be today. I was at the dentist recently. A softly shaped guy, fifty-ish, came into the waiting room wearing an avalanche of Gucci. Shoes, pants, shirt, and bag were all bright colors and busy patterns. He looked like he stepped on a Gilt.com minefield. If I saw him at an art opening, I would assume he was a painter from Romania. This was a lot of Gucci to wear to a teeth cleaning.

Age shouldn't diminish our appeal or limit our choices. But after a decade of Tom Jones–inspired sexy-man style, even Tom Ford buttons his shirt now. As Valerie Cherish said on *The Comeback*, "I don't need to see that!"

There was some chatter in the press in August 2019 that Tom Ford offered to give Mayor Pete a style-over. Mayor Pete smartly declined. I don't know what Tom had in mind for Mayor Pete, but I had a horrible image of Pete hitting the debate stage in a too-tightly-tailored black suit, too-pointy shoes, and a white shirt unbuttoned to the nipple line. For Pete to stay authentic, fashion should remain a spectator sport for him too. Mayor Pete is not a Tom Ford dreamboat. But he is a dream candidate. He does not need to make anyone's best-dressed list. We love him just for the way he thinks.

I approach my closet this way: I never know whom I'm going to meet today. Because fashion can speak louder than words, in ways both positive and negative, I always want that person to meet the best, most authentic version of me. It's why politicians, news anchors, and late-night TV hosts find their camera-ready uniform and stick with it. They are always who you want them to be.

If you use fashion to get attention, be careful of the flies you attract. When you reach a certain age, if a young man or woman finds you irresistibly sexy, they probably don't fantasize about what they'll do with your naked body; they dream about what they can do with your Amex.

"ALEC BALDWIN LOOKS..."

"...So old."

"...kind of crazy."

"...good. He's definitely slimmed down."

"...limpy. He limps now. What is that?"

"...so happy whenever I see him with his kids."

"...so fat."

"...yeah, but normal fat. Like middle-aged guy fat."

"...remember how hot he was in *Working Girl*!"

"...maybe he's overdue for Botox."

Oh, Alec. The price of fame. Everyone has something to say about you.

Alec Baldwin lives out east. He's around. At the beach with one of his many babies. Hanging in Amagansett Square with his kids. Out to dinner with friends. He hosts film screenings and moderates panel discussions at Guild Hall. Sometimes looking good. Sometimes looking like me when I walk the dog.

Yep. Stars—they're just like us.

He says "hey" and sometimes offers up random small talk. When I see him, he seems to just be a guy trying to live his life in the way we all do. I guess people are always surprised when movie stars don't always look like movie stars.

If you're famous or have any kind of notoriety, once you step outside your front door, there is never a moment that belongs just to you. I've lived in East Hampton, New York City, and Santa Monica—all three are hot spots for celebrity sightings. Here's what I've overheard:

"Hugh Jackman does not look like Wolverine."

"Huma Abedin has absolutely no right dating Bradley Cooper." (Not sure that rumor was ever true, but I wanted it to be fact.)

"Meryl Streep looks like a piano teacher."

"Sharon Stone walks down the street dodging imaginary paparazzi."

"Susan Sarandon looks like someone you'd see at your fortieth reunion."

"George Clooney makes Daniel Craig look meh."

"Is Mariah Carey the new Mae West?"

"Taye Diggs is so cool, he's almost too cool. It's almost annoying."

"Javier is everything you want a man to be."

"I just saw Bill Clinton in Soho. Somebody has to ask the question, 'Why did all these women want to fuck him?'"

"SNL hot is not real-world hot. Case in point: Colin Jost is not cute enough to even be in a boy band."

I sometimes crossed paths with Alec Baldwin outside the yoga studio. Here's my assessment: Alec Baldwin looks free!

I get the sense that Alec doesn't care what he looks like and definitely doesn't care what we have to say about him. In spite of all of his negative headlines and a few self-inflicted dramas, Alec just seems to be going along as best he can.

I always arrive early at yoga so I claim "my spot"—a corner near the windows that overlook the square. The first time I saw Alec, I cartwheeled up from a triangle pose into a Warrior 2 position. As my gaze followed my right arm out into the summer morning, it was like a painting, *Sunday in the Square with Alec*. All sorts of people doing their thing, including Alec and one or three of his kids. I wondered, *How does he do it? Conjure up that much energy at his age?* He was in his own joyful world, unaware of the people who spent more time watching the *30 Rock* guy than watching their own kids.

Other people's worlds puncture our world every day. Before Steve gave us the iPhone, we lived in a smaller universe. We knew our neighbors, office mates and some friends from childhood. Maybe you had buddies at the barbershop or shared smiles with other families at church. If you set out for a life in the big city, even the onslaught of fresh faces in elevators, buses, bars and gyms eventually settle into a familiar routine, a comfortable sameness. But now, almost like *Bewitched*, our phone transports us into other people's lives. We meet people who share their outfit of the day, renovation journeys, body transformations, life hacks, travel tips or a random duet with Idina Menzel. There's the mom who dances for us and the shirtless hunk who bakes but doesn't gain an ounce. Who are they? Is everyone's day more exciting, fun or interesting than mine? I waste the most psychic energy on the people who share their outfit of the day. I get lost wondering where they're going. And where they're going dressed like that? And does anybody just stay home anymore? And here I am, sharing my life with you. And maybe you're wondering how I have the time to go to yoga and then navel gaze at my own life.

"We should all meet up in downward dog."

Yogi's talking to me. I'm a few moves behind the class.

I need to get back to my world.

Alec inspired me to not give a shit about other people's expectations. Even if you look like you're fresh out of an asylum, get up, get out, and enjoy the damn day. And when you're out there, be in *your* world. That's where your life is happening.

Yoga helped rewire my brain. If you appreciate what you get, not what you don't get, chances are pretty good your world is big enough.

"I NEED A NEW BRAND!"

Early fall.

One of the miracle mornings. Cool air. Warm sun. Makes you think, *Yeah—there's a god.*

I'm headed to my car after a Monday class.

"You teach at Parsons?"

I turn. There's a woman in her late fifties. She's plain and pretty. There's nothing about her that tells me who she is or who she might have been. She's just there, looking like her yoga mat is her only friend.

"Oh—yeah—yes. I do. Teach."

"My daughter's thinking about Parsons. What do you teach?"

"Branding and Marketing."

"Oh—should I hire you? I need a new brand."

Oh no—another person with a budget of nothing.

"What's your business?"

"No—for me. My kids are always talking about their personal brands. Sometimes, they sound like *Mad Men*."

"It's social media. The AK generation."

"I thought my kids were Gen Z."

"AK—After Kardashian. They sell themselves. They are their own product."

I try out this bit of cleverness I've been kicking around: "If Einstein were around, he'd say $E=if^2$; energy equals image times the volume of followers squared. Followers are your currency."

She has no interest in what I just said. "Well, I don't need followers. I just need a new me."

To myself: *Why am I engaging in this conversation?*

This chitchat is about to get very personal. I can tell. Maybe too personal.

"Ever feel like you're at the departure gate waiting for your plane, but there's no destination or flight information? Ever since my divorce, that's me. Going nowhere."

She sees me searching for my line in this dialogue.

"It's been five years. Glad he's in the past, but when I look in the mirror, I see what everybody else sees: a divorced, middle-aged woman. I'm a dime a dozen out here. Case in point: This is the first conversation you and I are having and already, I'm talking about my divorce."

My thought exactly.

She didn't seem angry. She didn't seem confused. She just seemed to be floating in an emotionless void.

I don't want to go too deep into this conversation. And I certainly don't want to have another slice of this conversation every Monday. I wish I had this book finished so I could give her a signed copy and she could work out all this stuff on her own.

Then I offer up my best sixty-second advice: "Stop using the word 'divorce.' Stop saying it. Stop thinking it. Stop being it. In your mind, 'divorce' is a negative word. Culturally, you know that it's synonymous with failure. I think divorce can be a confident, empowered decision, good for everyone involved. Yes—even the kids. Don't 'be' your past. Be you now."

"I have to think about what you just said. What that means."

"You know, branding is not a drive-through business."

"You know, you should do a workshop. Half that class is divorced."

"Oh—didn't know."

"Seriously? You don't see the numbness in their eyes?"

"No. I look at you, I look at them, I just see yogis. That's why I say 'be you now.' People don't want to become friends with your past."

She seems to correct me. Or verbally tase me. She twists her mouth and eyes at the same time. "Be here now."

"What?"

"The book—*Be Here Now*."

"What book?"

"It's the seminal book on yoga and spirituality."

"Okay. Yes. Then, that. That should be your strategy."

"You've got to read that book. But it's good to be a little high when you read it. In many ways, it's a lot of what you said."

"Okay—well, thanks. I guess I'll see you next week."

"By the way, you're nicer than I thought you would be."

"What! Why? What?"

"You never smile."

"No. Never have. My personal brand is not smiley."

"Is that on purpose?"

"I don't like my teeth." I castigate myself, *Why am I telling her this? Why am I still talking to her?*

"Invisalign." She smiles a very nice smile that contradicts her energy. "Like they say in there"—nodding toward the yoga studio—"organize your face."

And so, I did. And after Invisalign, I smile more.

After yoga, I smile more.

It feels like a rebrand.

"THAT'S THAT."

It's done.

I wrote a book.

My relief just evaporated.

New alarms sound in the distance.

There's a new squirrel running around inside my head.

It's that question: "Now what?"

Actually, this squirrel sounds like a challenge.

Am I going to let someone read this?

Will I submit it somewhere? An agent? A publisher?

Am I open to being judged?

If you're reading this, then I've got an answer to "What's new?"

If you're reading this, thank you.

Your time is important. Hopefully this book will help you make the most of it.

I've often introduced client presentations with this slide:

Brand reinvention requires an openness to something new.

A blank slate.

A fresh start.

A story where past is prologue.

I approach my work assuming I know absolutely nothing.

But I also know that every story starts by discovering what *is* and what's *possible.*

What *was* is information, but what's ahead is always more interesting.

I went back to yoga in a riptide of doubt, uncertainty, and confusion.

I started this book in a similar state of mind.

Could I turn these undisciplined pages of randomness into a book?

What shape or form will it take?

Where was I in my shift from then to now?

I was idling at that intersection of trepidation and regret.

I started to push some thoughts onto a page, moving forward without knowing where I was going.

And that's always a good thing to do.

You don't have to write a book, but you want to find your new story.

Start with my essential question: "Who?"

"Who am I?"

"And what *exactly* are those squirrels running around in my head?"

It's been ten years since I started back at yoga.

Obviously, I'm ten years older.

If I didn't have yoga, I think I'd feel twenty years older.

Now—when I'm in the room, when I'm on my mat—it's not a replacement for running. It's a bit like church—it's the place I replenish my good energy.

Hands assume the prayer position in front of the sternum.

Thank the teacher within.

Namaste.

THE BLAH, BLAH, BLAH ABOUT ME

In case you haven't had enough.

"WHO AM I ANYWAY?"

This chapter is all about me. To be honest, you can skip this chapter if you want to. If you're busy, impatient, or in desperate need of your next you, you're done. You don't have to read another word.

I hear you. Trust me, I've spent enough time with myself to know I'm not that interesting. But here's my story in case you're interested.

The headline on my LinkedIn profile reads:

STRATEGIC LEADER | GLOBAL BRAND STEWARD | BOARD CHAIR | PROFESSOR

In my mind, the "real me" is the "twenty-years-ago me." That's me steeped in the world of branding and marketing, working to find the brand's story that's real and relevant and transforms curious consumers into dedicated customers. That me is in London, Madrid, or Paris, presenting a new campaign to the European marketing team. Or I'm in LA, it's nine in the evening, and New York is finally going to bed. I go to the bar at Casa del Mar for a cocktail and some random chitchat with a few tanked-up frequent flyers. Honestly, I'm there for the chips.

But those *were* the days. That's not me anymore.

Every now and then, I miss him. Not because everything about me was younger, but because I always felt that I was where I needed to be. I have more time now, but it can feel untethered.

We all miss something of our former selves. Like smoking. If you ever smoked, you are never a nonsmoker. You are forever a smoker who is currently not smoking.

I'm a sixty-something gay white male, teaching one marketing course each semester at Parsons. I spend time doing downward dogs, playing Rummikub, and trying to get comfortable "playing the net" on the pickleball court. As I write that, I hear me say, "My story is irrelevant."

I hear you say, "How can your cisgendered, privileged perspective give me any insight into me?"

Marketing requires a facility for speaking to universal truths and shared experiences.

I didn't drink tequila, but I did help Jose Cuervo add over one million cases to their annual sales.

I'm not a bodybuilder, but after four years making ads for GNC, I know the power of creatine.

I worked on the launch of Goop but never once had the need to steam a vagina.

The yogisms I share aren't mine, but I know they served as my GPS for navigating a weird, squishy, undefined time in my life.

In my business, I spend 99 percent of my time talking to clients about them. Their needs, desires, and "absolute imperatives." For me—a man who doesn't naturally share—I am in the perfect job. People love to listen to me talk to them about them.

My social media profile is nonexistent. Writing this book—sharing bits of me—feels like doing my own appendectomy equipped only with guidance from the surgical team at *General Hospital.* Typically, "essayists" come with some sort of impressive credentials. I haven't written a syndicated column. I don't have a celebrated TED Talk. I'm not the voice of a wildly popular podcast that can generate a built-in audience for this book. However, both personally and professionally, I've had to mull lots of stuff over and over in my head. My work requires a trained ear. Listening skills. As a marketer, I carefully consider client objectives, consumer motivations, functional obstacles, and emotional hurdles that challenge potential customers.

Friends have always sought my perspective on career, relationships, family, travel, restaurants, and gifting ideas. I've been known to know a thing or two. I've been called a "great suss-er," the person who figures out where to go and what to do before it becomes a "thing." When I travel, I search out the best coffee shops. The best coffee will always be found in neighborhoods with the most interesting people. The creative class demands superior coffee. And they'll pay for good coffee. Wherever you find overpriced coffee, you'll find equally indulgent shopping and overpriced restaurants with chic interiors and cool vibes.

I teach my students to actively listen. To always be the first to hear thunder. Waiting in an airport lounge, I can spot an interesting conversation that's worth overhearing. Like a dog picking up the scent of a chicken bone, I can sense people who probably know a thing or two worth knowing.

Because my network of friends has always included artists, designers, theater people, and academics, I've got lots of tentacles that reach into the fringes of culture. They've led me into uncharted waters. I love experiences in their pure state—that time just before they're "discovered," just before the next wave of "culture consumers" shows up at the insistence of *Time Out* magazine.

My EQ (emotional intelligence) seems to be well above average. I was raised under a cloud of myth. I credit my dysfunctional family, Catholic upbringing, and Jesuit education for my hyperdeveloped bullshit meter.

The Sisters of Mercy loved to terrorize children in school uniforms with their own brand of crazy. Until about ten years ago, I was a nail biter. In second grade, a despotic nun chided me with the parable of the fingernail bag. I assume religious scholars know what I'm talking about. Somewhere in the Old Testament, Sister Theodora found evidence that god made us with a fingernail bag in our stomach. Miraculously, fingernails go directly into this single-use sack. When it reaches full capacity, the fingernail bag explodes and all of the fingernails stab the evil nail biters from the inside out.

At seven years old, I was already suspicious of nuns and priests. Knowingly, at my annual checkup, I asked my pediatrician to check my fingernail bag. As I suspected, Dr. Spitz assured me that there was no fingernail bag. Proof: Nuns lie! And if nuns lie, then everybody lies. From that day forward, nothing was going to come between me and my fingers. Good Catholics are trapped by guilt. Bad Catholics receive the gift of irony. I remained obedient, but I was never an unquestioning sheep. I knew I would always seek the truth. I was born to color outside the lines. And I was going to live in New York.

I grew up when being gay in high school wasn't a "we love you no matter what" thing. My protective instinct demanded a keen sense of observation. I assessed emotional and behavioral motivations. I wasn't living my own truth, so to divert attention from myself, I became the best friend of anyone who needed someone to listen. To this day, I'm pretty good at seeing through the human shields that often hide a person's truth. Because my generation of gay people perfected the art of deflection, I always thought being a good listener was a gay superpower. Now that many young people are free to fly their own flag, do they still develop the art of listening? Will the "gay best friend" still be the go-to shoulder to cry on? Will closeted gay boys always fall in love with movies because it's their only way to live out romantic fantasies?

Splendor in the Grass was my awakening. I loved this movie. It popped up on TV a lot at the age when I first felt the heat of physical attraction. I'm not sure if I recognized my attraction to Warren Beatty, but, just like Natalie Wood, I knew I wanted to be bat-shit crazy in love. I wasn't sure what I was supposed to be craving, but I knew she wanted something way beyond just going steady. Watching that movie, I knew that once I lost my mind to first love, my life would heat up. I was starting to simmer.

It begs the question we all have: "If I was born in a different time or place, who would I be now?"

Fortunately, personal reinvention is your opportunity to be born of this time and place in your life.

I've made my living being the gay best friend brands can lean on. When they're not at their best, they call me. They talk. I listen. They might be unhappy, scared, nervous, or confused. They can share their secrets, like, "Sales suck!" or "The research on the new product is a fucking disaster!" Through strategic and creative conversations, I'm able to provide advice that can improve their relationships with internal staff and external customers. It's really not all that different than helping the prom queen understand that when the prom king said, "I love you," in the back of his brother's van, he was talking to her boobs. Anyone who attended Phillipsburg Catholic High School: there are no real prom queens implicated in this metaphor.

I'm no longer the ECD (Executive Creative Director) of Arnell Group. I'm no longer Global Creative Director for Maybelline New York. I'm no longer the Board Chair of The Trevor Project.

The minute you leave a position, the identity that comes with your title evaporates. Today, I'm none of the things that made it easier to introduce myself. I am a guy with a dog, a lot of sun spots, and some really nice sweaters.

Most people know me as a marketer. They don't know that there was another me: a screenwriter with promise. I practice what I preach—I don't always share my past because it isn't what defines me today.

Sure, I was a writer in Los Angeles for much of the '90s. In some ways, I can't remember myself from back then. The memories are blurred. I was so preoccupied with the business (which you have to be) that rather than live my life, I just existed in it.

I was a hip-pocket client at CAA, had a contract at Disney, and got a little work in sitcoms. I had an original screenplay set up at Warner Bros. The film was fast tracked with Joel Schumacher attached as executive producer. We had meetings on the set of *Batman*, which he was directing. I met George Clooney in his Batman costume. I'm certain that George has no memory of that day, but that could be the highlight of my career in the entertainment business. George was the Batman with nipples.

I loved living in Los Angeles. I went to a lot of movies. That was how I passed the time waiting for agents to call. Back then, if you wanted to see a movie, you had to go to the theater. Or wait forever for a DVD release. I would go to the first show in the morning, typically around 10:30 a.m. or 11:00 a.m. That allowed me to be home in the afternoon.

My job was to stare at the phone and wait for my agents to maybe, hopefully, call me back. I wish I was starting out in Hollywood today; with cell phones, you have the freedom to go anywhere and wait for your agent *not* to call. You can go to the movies in the afternoon if you want to. That's not just progress; that qualifies as humanitarian relief.

I was far from A-list, but I always had something that seemed hopeful. For the most part, I woke up every day with a career-defining and life-changing possibility dangling in front of me. In Hollywood, hope is a maintenance drug. Hope is better than nothing, even if nothing ever really happens.

If you're reading this, then this book has been published. With that, I can call myself a writer. Again. I've found a new title. A new story. And I've proven my point: No matter what age you are, no matter what muddle you might be slogging through, you can rewrite your story. If you think you have ten good years ahead of you, you can still set your world on fire.

ACKNOWLEDGMENTS

All my yogis who have guided me with inspiration and magical corrections: there are so many of you but Lisa, Jimmy, Frances, and Cheryl have been my A-team. And Jolie, who has always greeted me with a welcoming smile.

My publisher, Deb Englander, who said "yes" to this first-timer with confidence and enthusiasm.

HB Steadham and Sterling Hooker whose keen eyes and insights turned my mess into a book. Caitlin Burdette who kept this process organized and moving forward.

Barb Aronica, for blowing up my pre-conceived notions and surprising me with a cover I love. Dan Chavkin for making me smile. Melanie Fleishman—my fellow culture vulture—who offered significant observations of an early draft. Meredith Wagner and Geralyn Lucas—for their creative intelligence. Roz Lippel, for her thoughtful guidance. Beth Kastner who influenced key decisions in the first draft. Michelle Meyercord, who listened to my "blah, blah, blah" and said, "You should write a book!" And she said it with an exclamation point.

Sara Arnell, for her generosity, always opening doors and creating opportunity for me.

Laura Ganter O'Brien, for transforming crazy into fun and Jeff Meier who made the torture hilarious.

Nan and Patricia, for being a big part of my story. Rob, for turning up the volume on life. Ingrid, for being Ingrid. Jorge and Lloyd, for decades of laughs. Tony, Tracy, MAZ, the C-Bums, and Sheila for their joyful enthusiasm. Eppy—because everybody should have an Eppy. And Wade, who has always been a great audience for my stories.

Professor Roger Mooney, who in my junior year at Boston College, offhandedly commented, "You know you're a writer." I guess Roger was right even if he was hoping for something a bit more erudite than *The S@#t I Heard at Yoga.*

The staff at Bookhampton for always knowing what I need to read next. Your local bookstore is the best place to feed your heart, mind and soul.

ABOUT THE AUTHOR

Who is this guy I've never heard of? Michael J. Norton did the LA thing: wrote sitcoms and sold screenplays. After a contract at Disney evaporated, his agent said, "You're okay. You're solid B-list." Although it beats the hell out of the D-list, the B-list is an ego-bruising slog once you plateau. Say goodbye to Hollywood—hello marketing!

Michael spent a few decades developing creative and business strategies for clients such as Maybelline, Toyota, LVMH, Jose Cuervo, the Guggenheim Museum, Samsung, Pepsi, Martha Stewart, a smattering of fashion brands, and the launch of GOOP.

Since 2015, he's been "Professor Norton," teaching marketing, branding, and public relations at Parsons School of Design. Michael has been appointed to several corporate and non-profit boards, including two terms as board chair of The Trevor Project.

Michael is an avid reader, pop culture addict, and a dedicated but wobbly yogi. He's also a devoted pickleball player and has the injuries to prove it.